NINJA PHOTOGRAPHY

How to Create an 'Attack System' for Making Images

MIX

Papper från ansvarsfulla källor

Paper from responsible sources

FSC® C105338

Cover photo: Uffe Berggren

Publisher: BoD – Books on Demand, Stockholm, Sverige
Printing: BoD – Books on Demand, Norderstedt, Tyskland
ISBN: 978-91-8007-000-3

Nothing is original. Steal from anywhere that resonates with inspiration or fuels your imagination. Devour old films, new films, music, books, paintings, photographs, poems, dreams, random conversations, architecture, bridges, street signs, trees, clouds, bodies of water, light and shadows. Select only things to steal from that speak directly to your soul. If you do this, your work (and theft) will be authentic. Authenticity is invaluable; originality is non-existent. And don't bother concealing your thievery – celebrate it if you feel like it. In any case, always remember what Jean-Luc Godard said: 'It's not where you take things from – it's where you take them to.'

Jim Jarmusch, MovieMaker Magazine #53 - Winter, January 22, 2004

Ninja Photography

NINJA PHOTOGRAPHY

How to Create an 'Attack System' for

Making Images

Uffe Berggren

Contents

Intro – Show, instruct and practice

Originally, these texts were aimed at trying to use traditional training methods derived from language studies, track & field, military training and martial arts, applying them to photography in order to describe a possible way of sharpening and honing your skills in photography. Why did I choose to point out these fields as examples of educational background? The answer is simply that they are fields I have some experience from.

The mantra used in this book is a very traditional educational method that could be summarized with the key words: *Show, instruct and practice*. It is nothing more to it, no fancy, secret tips. It is just down to earth honest hard work that will make you better at anything you do.There are no secret paths towards greater proficiency. I would argue that it is all about having some guidelines and keep on practicing.

- You will be shown a way, or several, to make images.
- You may need some hints on what NOT to do.
- You practice, trying to apply what you have just been taught.

Still photography is about capturing the essence of something going on. It might be a slow process, or it might be trying to capture an image of a very complicated series of events occurring in some athletic game like soccer, track & field, or martial arts. If we want to capture ONE image from these events with some degree of interest for others it is possibly about understanding the game.

Still photography is, to some extent, also about finding the "exotic" in everyday life, that thing that is chafing your perception, like the 'punctum' Roland Barthes talks about. It is there, and it is up to you to find it within your everyday life, without going to places that unconditionally will give you some images of 'exotic' views in one way or the other. You should not make the mistake of believing that because you haven't seen your image earlier that it in general is an 'exotic' image. The big challenge is to find the 'exotic' in your everyday environment.

What stands out might be about something that has a 'hidden' shape in the form of 'perspective lines' that traverse the image in some spectacular manner when you discover them. Until then they are living in obscurity and appear to be 'ordinary', but when you expose them, they stand out in a self-explanatory way. You have made an interesting image and your surroundings seem to be more spectacular than before.

Skip the 'canned photography'

One last reminder about what is not the 'real' interesting photography. In the world of big game (and fowl) hunting there has appeared a concept called 'canned hunting'. In order to get hold of trophy's the hunters set out to kill the game within a confined area. I reckon it is a way of speeding up the hunt. At least it will up the odds for the hunter to get lucky. Of course it is not only other hunters who frown upon this manner of hunting, the animal welfare advocacy groups are not so keen on it either.

I advocate making images in the area where you live, digging deeper than ever, when you try to wring some new perspectives off from the streets you walk every day. So, you might guess where I am going with this.

Travelling to new locations to make images are not really making 'fresh' or, 'interesting' images. If you travel to Habana, Mexico City, Paris, Berlin, Amsterdam or Tokyo in order to make more 'interesting' images, the result will rarely be more 'interesting' images. What you make are images that might seem to be novel, or fresh, to you, but in all honesty, you have just added some 'exotism' that dupe you into thinking that your images are 'more interesting', or 'better' than the ones you do on your way to the grocery shop back home.

This way to fool yourself into thinking that you suddenly make a whole lot better images is almost as weak as the genre of 'Street portraits' in street photography. If you strike up a conversation with an individual in order to get him/her to pose, the whole idea is about setting up individuals in order to take the picture. If you then crop that image too hard, it could be one of your friends in your hallway, since you cannot detect any street background. Leave that to the people who lie to go on staging their photography. If you are interested in making images of the 'theatricality' in the city, it is a no-brainer that you should never ever stage your images. Okay, you might stage them in that capacity that you try to use a certain background, a special wall, building or doorway. You might be said to have staged your images by just choosing the moment you open the shutter. But, never ever stage your images more than that.

Snapping Pictures, or Making Images

What do you aim at with your photographic images? Are you trying to express some ideas, are you just trying to catch "life" or are you even more devoid of real aims? You will get more out of your photography if you set your own goals. One way to systemize your routine is to create "projects". One project might be to see to it that there are shadows as a showcase of the principal content in your photograph. You might make images of almost anything in the world and turn image series of it into a 'concept'. Examples are: "couples regarding each other", "back-lit scenes in general" or "tourists consulting a map". Whatever you might come up with as a good "concept" will do as a basic theme for your project. The manner in which you set up your 'concepts' will influence your photographic output. The physical world is out there to be turned into images.

The wise photographer creates a lot of basic themes. Sometimes the themes will come to you, they will in that sense create themselves, but you have to be open to accept them and not refuse them. You might discover that you want a couple of images of people eating in the street. Try to make a 'project' out of that. Don't be so hard on yourself at the very beginning of your project. You will get new insights that you have created a new concept, since this is a scenery that you can foresee a lot of coming in variations.

Basically it is all about making the images you want to make and sorting them along the ideas that you have about them. Looking at images "before" they really are images, i.e. finished "products" if you like, is hard, since you might not really have thought them through thoroughly enough to even know yourself what the images are expressing. You are, in a way, discovering what kind of images you are making.

At times the concepts will have been out there long before you realize that they might be treated as concepts. You might suddenly realize that you have a lot of images of traffic signs that have been altered by somebody with a felt marker or spray can. "The Public Change" is a concept as good as any. You might even divide it into sub-categories. In that manner you might, over time, create a lot of subgroups, and that might be a good thing. You will acquire a sense of trying to fill gaps in the "collections" of the subgroups. Perhaps that will lead you into discovering new themes.

Bear in mind that when you have first identified a "group" or a "concept" you will see them more clearly. You might even be surprised over the fact that you haven't noticed them before, since you realize that what you now call "concepts" really are images that have been out there for the making for a very long time. It is when you started thinking of them with a "label" that they became visible to you. That insight is a good one, since it means that it is a lot of images out there only waiting to be categorized. They are at arm's length away. You just have to get out there with your camera. It does not mean that you have to travel to a distant location, your concepts might help you to make your images anywhere.

You will be aided in your quest for "meaning" by your own sorting of your images into the subgroups of your "concepts". You will feel no urge to baptize your images with any name. They will stand alone without any title or caption, since you have already loaded them with content and stories. Don't write captions that describe what the viewer might see in an image. That is for the future curators of your photographic heritage to do in order to be able to archive your photographic images. If you need a caption to stay on the decent side of "good taste", or to explain it, your picture isn't good enough.

The aim, using aids like "concepts" or any labels for your pictorial material, is to broaden your vision on your objects. Does this belong within your categories, or has it no chance in belonging in any of the old ones? Then you have to make yet other categories.

This means that you will be systemizing your creation of images. Please, pay attention to that categories may be made to transcend geography, i.e., images made at the same location do not necessarily have to be categorized together. It is your "concept" that is the guideline with regard to your classification system. Let us imagine that one of your concepts is "darkness". That label means that you can sort any image with dominating dark areas into the category, but even images with some part "darkness" like a car tire against a white sandy beach may also belong in this category.

You will as time passes invent your own 'content' for your pictures looking at them and comparing them to other images you have made. You might discover that some of them are filled with similar ideas and forms.

When trying to match your images in categories you will have a lot of fun and steadily grow new insights.

Systematically sorting your images along themes or concepts will teach you to look at your images in a whole new way. Instead of looking at them one picture at a time, you will have the opportunity to try to group them in a bundle with some kind of traits making them related to one another. That will indeed help you with taking a close look at your own work. In a manner of speaking you will compete with your own images and make your conclusions from that comparison. Over time, some images might be sorted along new criteria. Since you discover that they belong more together with images that you hadn't sorted them with to begin with.

Basic tip

The manner in which you handle your equipment will have an impact on your images. Or, rather, it will be instrumental in your ability to capture the motifs that appear in front of your as you walk through your neighborhood. Be sure to have your camera ready to shoot at all times! Bringing a camera is not enough, you have to wear it in its strap around your neck or, in your hand, otherwise you will not be prepared to shoot when your moment manifests itself. You have to prepare your gear before you leave your house. That means that you should see to it that your batteries are alive and kicking, you ought to check your memory card for space. You won't appreciate to find yourself in the situation of being forced to delete images from it during your shoot. So, check your batteries and memory card before you leave home.

In this part some things like categorizing images and labelling them have been discussed. Some of the main features discussed above are:

- sort your images in folders according to 'themes'
- don't label your images with captions, or titles

Steps in your development

You might experience an initial giant leap forwards when you imagine, or at least get the feeling, that you are looking at the same image over and over again, even if the pictures appear to be the result of several individual exposures. Don't let yourself become confused by the similarities you encounter at first, since within that range of similarity lies an intense range of differences.

Let us suppose that your collection of images seem to show a diverse view of some aspect of life. You might have made a lot of images on a series of separate occasions when you have watched people standing in line in front of a kiosk in the street. Study each and every one of these pictures, looking for the story hiding in them: are there connections between people, are there textures that seem exiting, may the viewer assume that something is going to happen or, has just taken place, and so on!

So, what about the ideas that will come to you while you are compiling your sets of pictures along with your concepts? Keep an open mind while making your pictures. Do not try to make them in the same manner someone else would. Being inspired by others is all right, but don't copy. Try to draw on what others have done, but add something. That is imperative. No one loves a copycat; you will not even respect yourself if your work is too close to the photographers who inspired you. Copying the work of others will make you feel like a cheater, so try to get inspired by others and take their ideas to a totally new level. Adding, or developing, some of your own ideas, and your own processing of your material will enhance your photography. In doing so you will become a much better photographer, one who stands on the shoulders of giants in order to become a giant yourself. We should learn from others, preferably people we don't hang out with! That kind of closeness might end up devastating. That is, the advice you will get under such circumstances are not to be trusted.

Trying to create images that are part of you will take a while, but don't cave in, you will get there, even if you really may despair at times along the road towards your own photographic language. Make certain to choose with care whom is allowed to criticize your work in such a manner that you really will listen. It is not certain that it is good to choose your partner, relative, colleague or friend to look hard at your photographic work. First of all, these persons may not at all be interested in your work. Secondly, they might perhaps not have the necessary knowledge and overview to say something constructive that will help you. They might be nice to you, and you might not need or deserve that. You'll need someone looking at your images with an eye for visual storytelling. That person must be willing to look at least some hundreds of your images. A smaller amount will not be enough as material for an assessment of your level of skill.

So, you have to look a lot (A LOT) at pictures. Not

just photographs, but also paintings, movies, graffiti, calligraphy or whatever form of images you can think of. You have to shower your eyes and brain with pictures. You have to get a lot of experience to become able to create your own pictures. Yes, some are talented and seem to make pictures effortlessly, but if you are not one of those fortunate individuals you have to do it the hard way and look at pictures trying to learn how to create your own images. That's the way you do your homework. You are not really incorporating them into the way you make your images.

If you imagine that you will get your act together in a couple of weeks, your ambitions are too low. real planning for the future skills and improvements ought to cover at least a year. In all other cases you're only trying out things you are interested in.

Doing is learning and watching is part of learning to find elements in your soon to be created pictures.

Exercise: This is an exercise you can do at home. The main objective is to incorporate some foreground and background into your shot. It is built on three levels, center, foreground and background. So, try to spot what is to be in the center of your image. Then look at the background, what do you see there? The step that often will kick life into your image is to find some foreground. Don't take the easy choice of incorporating a spectacular back drop. Aim at including everyday backdrops. You don't want the backdrops becoming the prime part of your image. Whatever your friends argue about juxtaposing, that part is not your image. Then you just focus on everyday occurrence in front of a spectacular background.

You have to elaborate on where you position your focus in your image. You might place it in the foreground, at the center or in the background. Try all three options and you will discover that your image will look very different depending on your choice of focus.

In this part some things like how you should think about a few things in order to make your images better have been discussed.

Some of the main features discussed above are:

- don't make use of juxtaposing with marvelous back drops too much, you will become dependent on this
- looking at a LOT of images from all fields of image making will make you a better photographer

Finding out what you want to say

As you make progress during your immersion into the world of visual arts you may start to wonder where your stories are in this disparate flow of stories and images. Yours might be about light contra darkness, shift of focus, blurriness, catching the "theater in the street" or "the happenings of nature". You might lean towards making images at events that someone else has staged – like festivals, concerts or the like in a more journalistic genre. Whatever you design or what method you use, someone has probably tried that variant earlier.

But don't you fret! The fact that someone already has tried a method, or style, really is good for you. If you can get hold of examples in books, or on the Internet, or elsewhere you may learn something and in the process you don't necessarily have to do the same mistakes as your predecessors. Mind you, you're supposed to gather ideas, not becoming a copy cat!

What is the story of a concept?

For starters, each individual image has to contain a story to be interesting for other people, probably even for the creator of the picture too. If you, as a viewer, are not intrigued by your own images, if you can't see the "riddle" in them (Roland Barthes called it "punctum") probably no-one else can either. If you get many "likes" in a group on social media it doesn't really mean that the image is a "good" image. All that those likes indicate is that you have reached the "main-stream" level within that particular group. Getting no likes means either that your picture is unique, or that it is lacking in so many ways that no one even bothers to comment. Okay, I'm exaggerating, but you get the main idea, creating images with, at least, some impact is a rather lonely activity. Sometimes I upload an image in some Facebook group that is actually what I regard as an "average" image, and to my amazement I get busloads of 'likes'. Don't I understand the 'greatness' of some of my images? Maybe, or maybe not. What is a great image to me does not necessarily have to be 'great' to anybody else. I lean towards regarding the 'story', 'punctum', or 'riddle' as the 'agency' of images. Agency has a lot to do with loading the images with traits that are recognizable within (or without) your own cultural surroundings.

That doesn't mean that you cannot have friend that are trying to do the same things as you yourself. You have that ambition in common and that ambition may prove to be fruitful! So, you might be a member of what David Riesman called "the lonely crowd" when he described the emerging American middle class during the 1950s.

Images may be argued to be about ideas that are described by turning them into lines, shadows, highlights and a spectrum of colors. That means that they are possible to turn into almost anything you might imagine. An idea is something that is created, we don't necessarily "have" ideas, we spawn them in order to create new solutions and we spawn new combinations of ideas when we least of all expect it. That is why the 'making' of images is important enough to really create a part of a really continuous flow of images.

It is very important to take good care of your ideas. Without them you will not create many photographs, not good ones, at least. You have to cultivate your ideas in order to be able to execute them in a manner that will render them a presentational form that is so good that others may comprehend their content. It would seem to be an easy task, but trust you me, it really isn't! Ignoring the complexity of images is, at the least, a major mistake,

You might say that images are driven by ideas. In the long run that indicates that without ideas backing your images you will end up producing a bunch of contentless, flat, hollow or empty images – at best replicas of someone else's ideas and work. You have better hurry up trying to come up with some ideas or you will fall behind. If idea is king, execution of the images is its shadow. Good ideas, good execution and good presentation is the rule of three that will make it possible for you to accomplish some great pictorial work. With a systematic approach you will make more "good" images over any given time span. The strategy to think constantly think about your images will help you getting around the worst trap of all – getting trapped by color alone. An image consists of content trapped inside what is seemingly "seen" in the picture. You have to combine the "content" with what is "shown" in the images. The two aspects will together become an awesome image. You have to bear in mind that the ideas are the basic content in the images. Without underlying ideas it doesn't matter what colors, focus or shades you have caught. There is a lot of technical aspects to making images. I don't mean only your camera's limitations, but rather the way you apply the capabilities of your camera and your ideas about images.

The pictures you have created so far in your life deserve that you take your time looking through them. Maybe you have already touched upon concepts that you can develop further? You might even see ideas surface on alternative pictures, images that you didn't expose at the moment you are out there taking them. Try figuring out why you didn't make the pictures you now understand that you could have made. Understanding why they were never exposed is a step further in understanding yourself as a photographer. This might perhaps be the first step in really getting to know what kind of pictures that make you tick and what kind of pictures you should avoid, since they don't do anything for you and/or your art.

You may stumble on surprising answers during the time your spent out there, in reality, making your images. If you have believed that your pictures of architecture are what you should see as your path it may come as a surprise to understand that you have created a number of impressing photographs of flowers and trees – they really get to you when you look at them a couple of years later. Even if they are your own images you tend to see them as rather good, since they seem to "tell" something.

It is at cross-roads like that you have to decide what is the most important. Is it to nourish the mental image of yourself as an architectural photographer or to do the best photographs that are possible for you, and are within the reach of your skills?

Maybe you have to abandon your architectural photography? Well, you don't have to abandon it all together, but you may have to allow for more time photographing flowers for example. Don't worry if it feels awkward at the beginning – it will perhaps change your outlook on photography as a whole. The more you learn about your new motifs, the more fun it will get!

It is like that with everything we commence doing – if we are lucky, we think it is becoming more and more fun as time goes. You may keep on doing your architectural shoots, but concentrate on the flowers and plants for a while. Or, you'll do both, because it is bound to push you into doing things towards an end just because you will keep your attention on its toes that way. If your heart is in the architectural photographs, don't deny what your heart is trying to tell you. Leave the flowers and plants to someone else and be happy and forever content doing your architectural photographs!

In this part some things like working according to

a systematic approach towards your image making and, the kind of motifs you choose to work with doesn't really matter have been discussed. Some of the main features discussed above are:

- try to focus on a number of select motifs
- you might find any combo of motifs might work for you

Where and how to shoot

The locations where you shoot your images, is there any importance in being picky about choosing them? The optimal case is if you are able to shoot your photographs anywhere. Even if the back-drop, or setting, might more or less DO a picture, it's not wise trying to create a style that is totally dependent on rare or exclusive geographical back drops.

If you choose to go down that lane you must ask yourself if you're incapable of doing photographs in an ordinary plain environment. I agree that some of nature's or certain cityscape's configuration do tend to make it possible to allow for doing more spectacular pictures than other locations. The awesome pictures you do there are dependent on that milieu and really does not tell if you yourself are a talented photographer or not. If you never attempt and learn how to execute, spectacular, pictures in a more everyday environment you have to ask yourself some questions:

- Do I see images before they are exposed?
- Do I need a lot of "preparation" to start shooting?
- Am I able to manipulate "ordinary" images into "spectacular" ones with image editing software?
- Does the image have to be straight?

Do images have to be in focus?

Do you make use of concepts like "the rule of thirds", or "the golden ratio"?

Before we start discussing what these questions imply and what we may do to get along with part of them, let us imagine an example: What if all photographers had the same equipment and there were no alternative settings to be done on the camera and the image editing software was just a manner of cropping or tidying the picture up. Would that mean that no awesome images were made in the future? Probably not. If there is a will to create images filled with stories, there is a way to see to it that those images are made.

Seeing images before they are exposed

A short-cut into creating "interesting" visual art is the capability to be able to "see" pictures before they are actually made, even before they are sketched. If you are able to imagine an image you will be able to visualize it and to hunt down the circumstances that are needed for it to become a reality. If you don't have any ideas before you go out shooting you are totally in the hands of circumstances beyond your control. But that is ever never the case, even the person thinking she's 'without ideas' do have ideas. When the photographer sets out to do, for example, street photography, she is prepared. Even if the ideas preceding this special shoot, might be ideas about how the light falls on a wall and a side walk. This is part of preparing, having some vague idea about light phenomena in the street that you want to include in your image or, to have dominating your picture. You will set out looking for that light during your walk around your city. So, there is nothing like being unprepared.

Keeping your toes on the line until you've fully executed the images you want to do is the most hazardous stage in the pursuit of interesting images. The images are out there, the only quest and problem is to bring them into the photographer's fishing net / memory card. It is like when you're fishing you have to know, at least it is smart to have a rough idea about, what you aim to catch. To some degree your attitude influences what kind of pictures you make. Your own state of mind will decide what kind of materials you bring home. Your state of mind is in analogy with when fishing, your bait and the hooks you're using. If you're not prepared there will no catch. So, your state of mind might be said to be the ground stones of the pictures you imagine you will capture on a special day or during a certain amount of time.

Whether your preconceptions of your images are "clear" or based on "intuition" they are a good thing for your photography. The thought that you could go out and create a picture like "red on yellow", "dog versus boy", "sadness" or even "things happening in the streets" is a good and hopeful one.

You will develop into a good photographer, introducing the handles you come up with!

"Preparation" before starting to shoot

Are you the kind of photographer who visits a location several times before actually even bringing a camera? Some photographers work that way, discovering or excavating a location, getting ideas about what to do there. They are coming back to check the light during different parts of the day, or even during the night. They are trying to decide whether the background colors will give them any ideas and they might want to decide whether this is a busy location with a lot of people and vehicle traffic. Busy might be good for some kinds of street photography, but not necessarily for other kinds of photography, depending on your visual taste and ideas.

Try not to rig your set in the old, and ordinary manner. Think through the set-up, do you really need a tripod, a handheld flash, LED-lighting and whatever more equipment? Try to make it simpler, just bring your favorite camera body and your favorite lens, leave the rest of your gear at home!

Your gains will primarily be that you will get ready to shoot much faster, you might catch the objects or events you are chasing in a simpler and more immediate fashion. That might lead to that you will make pictures of many more targets and in the long run you will have a lot of potential images to work with in your image manipulation software. There are of course times and images that will need a lot of rigging, but you have to spend some time working with less equipment in order to be able to see the possibilities with using less equipment, and you will come closer to your motifs. Try the more lightweight style for a while and play during your photographic endeavors! More play and less preparation! Use a smaller bag with equipment on your missions. Make it light and easy to become a fast moving, fast creating and fast recuperating photographer!

Working "ordinary" images into "spectacular"

Whatever image editing software you ordinarily use, you have to decide, and know, you are going to use it. If you have large revenues from your pictures you may choose to use state-of-the-art brand name software. But if you want to use photography as a hobby which is less complex than running a photographic business you will look for free software like Gimp and DarkTable. There are others out there, but these two are the ones I have some experience of.

Like with the hardware there is no universal "best" software. If all editing you do is straightening the images, applying some unsharp mask and edit in size you do not need software that can do a lot of stuff you never will use. If you, in the future, get far more ambitious in that area, then it is perhaps time for a more serious investment in heavy duty software.

There is no need to pay for stuff that you don't intend to use. We all tend to reason that it is good to have more capacity than we need, but is that really a true statement? Does the overcapacity drive us towards playing around instead of working with some clear-cut ideas that we really want to develop further? This is possibly due to that you haven't really set your mind to what kind of images you want to make.

It is easy to get lost when you encounter all the possibilities that are accessible in both hardware and software. So, you had better do with a strategy to bridge and narrow down all the possibilities. Rather than getting totally lost among the choices you are forced to do at the time. To narrow them down a bit will benefit your future photography. It might even get you so focused that you will heighten your capacity quite a bit. You have better really learn the software of your choice. Your experimenting ought to have some goals, or else you will find yourself just taking chances during your manipulation of your images. You might even find yourself using some effects for all the wrong reasons.

Does the picture have to be straight?

No. There are no "have to's". Your images don't have to "be" in any special way, the most important thing is that they engage the viewer. You can practice teaching your images telling a story just by making up a story around the pictures. The story might evolve within the frame of the picture, or, use your picture as a stepping stone and take off from what your image suggests. As you go along, you will come to develop a gut feeling that shows you the way.

If it is hard to tell a story about your picture maybe

it has no story within itself. Don't get disappointed, this could be the start of something, maybe even a story. The story doesn't have to be fixed in the photograph, but the picture must in some way be instrumental in transmitting the story. If they don't, why bother even exposing them? Don't regard your photography like it is something you are just playing around with, relaxing from the pressures of work or trying to fill up your days as retired. That doesn't count, photography is NEVER a pastime! You don't make pictures to relax. You make images trying to make a statement about our time and age. You want to describe what is happening around you. Whether you do that to immortalize your neighbor in your back yard or by making pictures of your latest kitten is irrelevant. That's what you are doing, nothing more to it, really!

The best advice to anyone endeavors in life really is: don't make it more complicated than you have to! There is always a minimum effort in doing something. If you land a bit above that minimum you are okay. You can make very good pictures with a camera with a 10 MP sensor, but to be on the safe side you preferable will use a camera with a sensor that executes pictures above 12 MP. Perfectly exposed pictures of this weight might be offset printed on paper in the size of A3 in 300 DPI. If you have the possibility to aquire a camera body getting over 24 MP, you're in the clear for some time ahead.

Do pictures have to be in focus?

No. And I'll tell you why. When we use our eye sight only part of what we see is in focus. We get the impression that all of our surroundings are in perfect focus. I guess that that result has to do with a delay in our brains interpretations of what the eyes are registering.

Thus the pictures you make definitely don't have to be entirely in focus. Some parts or, at least, one part has to be in focus, otherwise you have just produced a generally "blurry" picture. That brand of pictures may have a place in the world, but they won't contain much of a story. The kind with only an inkling of a start on a story, but they might, on the other hand, appear tremendously intriguing, due to the fact that they produce a story in our heads. That means that we, as spectators, have started to solve the "riddle" in the picture. What surrounds the sharp detail, what is it a part of? Are the details in the form something that could be a part of a story?

The difference between the clear-cut parts and the more diffuse ones will turn your picture into a riddle for the viewer and hence start the hunt for the possible answer to the riddle. Remember that in this context, the riddle is everything! An image that is too plain or ordinary, made straight off from your target will rarely do anything for the spectator. It will just leave the spectator with a feeling of nothingness. You wouldn't want that, would you?

The rule of thirds and the golden ratio

An easy way to make your images more "composed" is to work with the rule of thirds and / or the golden ratio. The rule of thirds is about partitioning your image in nine equally large rectangles, or squares, depending on whether you use you use a rectangular or square format for your images. Check the menu of your camera to use the grid of helplines that will show on your camera screen. The basics of using this grid is to place something in your motif at the crossing of two lines. You don't have to use all the nine spots where the hairlines are crossing. One will be enough to advance your composing skills. Now you are using the rule of thirds. The golden ratio is a more complex way of checking your images composition wise.

Whenever you decide to make a "good" picture, just relax and let your eyes lead you to whatever they see. Often, they have seen more in a motif than your brain, at this moment, is ready to perceive, there might be a story in what you are watching, you just haven't noticed it yet.

Be patient, you will find motifs that are possible documenting with your camera. When in doubt, let the shutter be opened, especially if you use digital technology. You might be sorry afterwards if you didn't open the shutter a couple of times. There are no more costs at the moment other than the time you spend making those frames.

Use the technology you have access to, i.e., the stuff you have already bought. I want you to try something new, check if some friend has access to that equipment, try to borrow it for a couple of days. Return it promptly! While you borrow the equipment you shall check it out and try to determine if it is something that could help you to acquire the pictures you have a notion of wanting to create. You will rather soon find out if the gear you test is something for you. A reminder; even if fish-eye-lenses in a manner of speaking may help you create intriguing pictures; the result is not a synonym to "good pictures". It is very easy to hop on a technology-driven style of images, but is it really what the story in the pictures is all about? Rather than settle for "effects", aim at making complex images. These are images that get the viewer thinking. If some of the viewers get lost in your image, then you're on to something.

My recommendation is to avoid technology-driven photography with results that are entirely relying of a specific lens or lighting. It is almost a no-no in the same category as traveling to faraway places to use a location in order to put some "awesomeness" into your images. If you rely on the fact that you cannot create pictures that are great in your own backyard you have to practice SEEING your own surroundings! That is one of the hardest lessons there is – to accomplish awesome pictures on a location that you are familiar with. That is an effect of the misunderstanding that you look at what's familiar. When in reality you don't!

Try this exercise! Sit down with a piece of paper and describe your own home, noting the color on carpets, walls and the rest. Are there any carpets in all rooms? What are the pictures on your walls depicting? I reckon that you will not get much of this description accurate. So, do you still think that you have LOOKED at your familiar location at the level that means that you really know what it looks like? You may be able to list the stuff you own, but will have problems giving the exact location of these items.

In the line of training it is always better to make a lot of pictures, i.e., practice a lot. When you practice you should try to make images you haven't tried to capture earlier. But you should also make a lot of pictures that you already know that you perform well in making. You have to practice what you are already good at, but practice more what you're not so good at. Unless you do that, you will never become better and a more advanced photographer in a much broader sense.

If you lean back and are content with your present level of proficiency the possibility is even that you will become less skilled than you once were. It seems like the ability to make a couple of awesome images each year is a skill that is ageing and fading very fast. You have to practice to keep being perfect!

So, you have to be on your toes, constantly trying to become even more skilled. Remember that pro photographers count on taking a couple of really good pictures each year. So you shouldn't let your mood sink if you won't even get one picture a year that is fabulous. You make you're living some other way I guess, that is probably why you are reading this.

If your ambition is to become a professional

photographer you have to reach a standard for all photographs you make that is above par. (Let's say ALL the images you let other people see shall be over par.) Since as a professional all the images you let other people see are a manner of marketing of your skills, you can't afford to allow others to see BAD pictures within the genre the images are published. So, beware of this, if you're looking for a new career be rather picky about what images you display for others to watch.

For everybody else, already with careers in other fields, my advice is to stick to that career if you're able to support your family by it. This is no career advice, but be aware that, for the most part, living on your photography is not that glamorous that you might imagine it to be.

Having photography as a hobby may be a bit glamorous though! No, I was just kidding! Even as a hobby photography is a lot about hard work, people questioning why you make photos and people in the streets trying to stop you from making photos. Some days it's like all the Karens of the world are out there, trying to stop you, or threatening to call the cops on you. Most common is that non photographers think that it is forbidden to snap pictures. That is very different, depending on the laws and regulations within different countries, Check what is allowed in your country, or on the location where you're going to shoot. There ARE discrepancies between regulations in different countries so search for what advice the national photography associations may offer on the subject. It's better to be safe than sorry.

Meanwhile I will return to the topic of the constant hunt for images. People who state that there is nothing to photograph shouldn't have been allowed to buy a camera in the first place! We live in a world full of motifs, but you should choose what motifs you make pictures of by yourself. It's no use making pictures of the Eiffel Tower if you have no new idea on what picture to create. The Eiffel Tower has been photographed by everyone who's ever been to Paris, France. If you have new ideas, go ahead!

It's a challenge that most things and sceneries around us has already been photographed and that it is hard to come up with novel ideas on how to make new images. You might succeed if you're able to use ideas used in previous photographs but give them a new twist. You make stuff with your image language with parts from fashion photography combined with traits from architectural photo or vice versa. It might even be wise to check out other crossover attacks, when making images in your usual surroundings. That transfer might appear as a new handle on the subject and appear to be a new twist on both sides. But beware! That novelty works only for a while!

The things we are trying to create pictures of are not necessarily the ones that in general we may regard as "photogenic". The real McCoy may be something completely different. The brush you use to clean your floor with, the tiles in the floor, or the bucket of water you carry to your hens.

The main idea is to really look at things in your surroundings, take close peeks at the stuff and people you are accustomed to. You might argue that you probably are so used to not looking at them since you're convinced that you know what they look like. You will discover, when you start looking at your partner, kids or neighbors is that they don't look like you remember them looking. There is a whole universe of possible pictures to be made right next to you! So, open your eyes and take a closer look!

Even buildings in your part of the world are worth a closer look. They don't look like you remember them looking. When you open your eyes and scout into the world around you will look differently at your surroundings. You will start to discover "interesting" shots waiting to be made all over the place. All you have to do is start letting "all" the images into your life.

Take a peek through your window from an angle you seldom use. Using frog's view, from above, straight up along a facade, or whatever angle you may come up with. If you always make your images standing straight up, with your camera covering your face, try to avoid that position for a while. You might discover other perspectives, like kneeling down, shooting from the hip, raise your arms with the camera above your head, and so on.

Look closely at your everyday environment! I reckon you will find images hidden there that will reveal themselves at a closer glance. Like I stated earlier: we think we know how things look around us, but we are wrong, so totally wrong. Take a look borrowing some stranger's gaze for some seconds and an entire new world will appear in front of your lens! You'll be amazed at what reveals itself in front of your eyes. The image-world hidden in your immediate vicinity will surprise you!

So, leave your beaten tracks for a while. Explore new track to follow, even in your own neighborhood. You will find new and fun ways to improve your photography. The run of the mill making of images should be overthrown and you try to start a new.

Imagine yourself as a visitor from another planet. What would you find interesting in this world? What would you then make images of? Where would you find stories to send to you home planet out there, what would you chose to show representing this alien world? You must, in a way, regard our everyday world as an alien supposedly would, so take a further look at it. Estranging yourself in that manner, you supposedly will gain new insights in how your world is constructed and might be turned into a photographic image. The way you your camera will be used will in a couple of hours have changed forever.

You will look at your world in a new manner. In a way, if you're so lucky, your new look-out at the world will change you forever. That might be a heavy gain for your stride as a photographer. You will "see" images in a way that will be different from your usual manner of just grabbing your camera and snap the pictures!

It is all about leaving the beaten tracks and venture into new ways of seeing. Once you are on a new track, you'll see a world of pictures you didn't know existed before. That is a comforting thought for your future photographing, I reckon that it will be a good thing for your ego too, when you venture into new areas and new motifs.

The continuous hunting for new motifs is your quest. Either you dig deeper into the kind of images you usually make, or you search for new hunting grounds. In either case, you will be surprised by what you find if you only dig deep enough. Some of that constant digging at the same location with apparently the same motifs will lead you into new grounds. I can't stress enough how much excitement and joy that journey might bring you. You probably will upgrade your pictures in the quest for the truly amazing ones that hard work and experimenting will earn you.

With every endeavor in life there is hard work required. You won't create awesome images just by following your usual path. The amazing pictures are credited by those individuals who look up from the usual trail and dare to look at the side, to the front, above or below the trail that everybody else is following. So, step outside your comfort zone and take your first steps into an exciting future for your photography! It might be scary to leave your comfort zone, but you will perhaps gain so much by taking the step out into the unknown that you will gain skills and confidence like never before. The great thing about that is that it will be done by you, and nobody else!

It is possible that you have to obtain new skills to lift your photography to a whole new level of proficiency, but you will be like the rest of us: if you're not learning new skills and try new ideas, you'll soon lose interest in your hobby. By learning more, you will change yourself, you might be a plumber or a financial advisor, but you are also a photographer. That is a very good thing. At least for you, perhaps for the people around you who might marvel over the stunning pictures someone they know can produce! Of course you will have a lot of fun when you are acquiring your new skills. Man seems to be designed to learn new skills, and that learning will make us feel comfortable and happy. Not knowing is not an especially happy place.

When we look back on our lives it seems like some of our happiest moments may relate to learning new stuff. The new things and skills we learn blends seamlessly with the rest of the stuff we know beforehand, so there is very hard to discover what was there from the beginning and what was recently added. Once you picked it up it is like a part of your personality and can't easily be separated from the person you were from the start.

So, the new knowledge you acquire will become a part of the essence that is you and you will not be able to tell where the borders between old and new lines will be drawn. That, of course, is a good thing, since that is really a part of who you are and not a clearly visible new add-on.

When you take a glance, make a reminder of who you were before and then on who you have become with your new skills, you'll be amazed by how alike they are, but yet, there is something new added to this present you, someone you were not before. You have added something through your exercises and your efforts to incorporate new skills to your repertoire. You have a possibility to become a photographer you never even thought you could become. In doing all the work yourself you have surpassed your old self, becoming someone you never thought you were able to become.

So, when you have mastered these new skills, you're a star now, or what? Not really, the learning process never stops. You will still have to acquire new skills and they will lead you even further away from the person you once were, who maybe thought that becoming a decent photographer comes easily? Or, that buying an expensive camera and lenses is all there is to it? When you have tried to learn new skills, acquired some of them, you see that you could do things with your camera that aren't described in its manual. You've learnt that and you see that you will have to learn even more. But now that doesn't bother you. Instead you see your shortcomings as possibilities to advance your skill level a whole lot more. You've become a photographer that grows, and given time will create some stunning images!

In this part some things like learning new skills and adapting new approaches have been discussed. Some of the main features discussed above are:

• The general acquisition of new approaches to photography, new motifs, new ways of looking.

• The Rule of Thirds and the Golden Ratio

Limitations

In order to become even more excellent at what you do, one thing to try is to limit yourself while doing it, as an exercise. It might have to do with your equipment, or the way that you act as a photographer. The most important thing is that you see to it that you never experience yourself as being a victim of circumstances, i.e. having to execute some shots within limitations due to the fact that your equipment really does not allow you to make the images you aspire to make. The limitations do, in general, come in the form of two aspects; the hardware limitations and the limitations in your mind about what is possible to do. We will explore this in the following pages.

Hardware limitations

It is important to clearly decide whether it is your gear that is the culprit for what you experience as your limitations, or if it is you that limit yourself. You might do exercises like for example, involving only using a wide angle lens, like the equivalent of a 35 mm standard lens (in most half frame cameras it will be somewhere between 18 and 22 mm). Spend a week shooting with that lens only (or the corresponding settings your lens may have) and really test its limitations and advantages. Try to outsmart the lens. Since you have no zoom you have to "zoom with your feet", i.e., take a step closer to your object. This kind of lens might have a slight distortive effect on horizontal and peripheral lines in the picture, especially off center (not really a fish-eye effect, but slightly in that direction). Check if you can use that effect in your pictures and try it out to do images where the "bending" tendency doesn't show until you use a ruler to check the picture. A very subtle effect, that is.

Try to shoot landscapes, portraits, sports pictures and the likes. You'll notice that there are benefits of making pictures in an environment that doesn't "suit" the lens. The result might be radically different compared to the result coming from you using a 18-55 mm lens (27-82 with the 1.6 coefficient). Maybe you'll have found something out that could be of use for you in your upcoming work as a photographer. Maybe you find that this is not your cup of tea. Don't despair, you will find out a lot by working with limitations in this manner. You will learn a lot about your equipment and a bit about your own style of photography. Understanding the limitations of your equipment will simultaneously teach you a lot about yourself.

Bring a flash if you own a separate one, otherwise use the built-in flash in your camera. Try to understand what the flash does for your pictures. If you have a separate flash with an extension-cord try to use it to angle the flash differently and notice what affects you obtain. Experiment thoroughly, it is through using the equipment when it doesn't matter that you'll learn what you might use it for in a "sharp" real-life situation.

When using the term "experiment" I really mean playing around with the flash, especially if you have a hand-held one. Move it around, having the camera set to sequence-mode and learn what happens when you make ten subsequent exposures, some with flash, and others without. You ought to try moving the camera and the flash separately, practice not moving your arms in a curved pattern. Study your results. Do you notice anything there, that you want to use? If you decide that it is not, please remember the results for future use, when you've changed your mind. If you are leaning towards "artsy" pictures, this is perhaps some of the technical stuff you should remember.

On moving the camera

I've already mentioned the moving of the camera, with a separate flash. It's easier to move only the camera, when you're exposing your pictures. You may like to do this when you're trying to "freeze" a moving vehicle speeding sideways in front of you. You might even use the zoom function while exposing the picture. Try that while using a tripod, then you just have to concentrate on the zooming in or out on your object. This is to ensure that you hold the camera still and just use the zoom function. When you manage this you will discover "zoom lines" in your pictures. Try it out.

When you're playing around with these functions,

remember to make wide turns, don't limit yourself while practicing, let things happen, let chance have its way during your photographic sessions, let things happen as they will happen. Keep track and be observant of what you are doing. You want to be able to repeat some of the stuff you create during these playful sessions at some later date.

Now, this is only one way to start. There are several others. Be creative when you practice. Play around with your equipment and your ideas. Try to decide what the pros and cons are, what are the limitations, does the method require a lot of light and thus will not work that well at dark nights? If you have problems handling a technique you like, maybe it's time to google that technique and get some help that way. Just being stubborn helps you a lot too!

Try to learn more

If you're searching for a special effect one way, described above, is basically trial-and-error. You might also consider taking classes in photography, but first visit your local library, check out what books they have on creating images in general, i.e., books on art in a wide sense, both traditional and more experimental. There you will have all the books you need to technically produce photographs, you'll find monographs on individual photographers, books on photography from a certain era, from different countries, etc. Don't overlook the opportunity to use the information in books. You will gather a lot of examples from the photographic industry, but there are a lot of older books that points to the basics concerning creation of pictures. That includes on painting and drawing. You might find them as PDFs on the Internet, but some you won't find there, but in the library.

Look at images, not only photographs. Look at people, horses, shadows, animals in general, cityscapes and of course, nature in general. You might think that you have it all covered. I beg to differ. I guarantee that you haven't watched all the images in the world that could have bearing on your work in photography. I even bet that you are aware of that. So, why don't you look at some more pictures? You won't ever never regret the time you spend doing it.

I would argue that even pictures that aren't to your taste might teach you something. Don't be afraid that you'll rumble into new field of photography. If that happens, so be it! I reckon that it happens for a reason and that reason is that you like the new field of photography too. Maybe even better than the field of photography you used to have as your favorite and inspiration. You just didn't know it yet.

I also reckon that when you add another field of interest, you will be getting better at creating pictures in your original field. Photography is always photography, i.e., following the laws of physics it always has to follow. No surprises there, even if some people argue that the differences between analog and digital photography make them two separate fields of art. Some people even argue that you can't be good using both techniques. But we don't believe that, do we?

We will shoot with our camera and trying to do

the best pictures we can at any given moment. There is no rocket science about it. Just o whole bunch of imagination at play.

There are possibilities to make some kind of rocket science of this, but that is not the main objective. The objective is to make good, interesting pictures.

But really, who wants to be pretentious? Doing pictures that tell a story and being content with that achievement? You don't have to really reach the stars, the journey you are partaking in is the thing to remember. If you advance your knowledgc about your equipment and learn how to use it making the photographs you want to shoot, that is an achievement! If others like what you are doing, great, but the acceptance from others will not really advance your photographic skills. What you learn and train for will absolutely do that in the long run.

As a rule the great giants historically within the photographic industry made do with far worse equipment than you have access to today without ruining yourself. So, there is nothing to whine about, just do your photography, hunting down those pictures that will change your world in the sense that after you've made those images you will never be the same individual again. That image created by you has the power to change your existence in its foundation, rearranging your mind and what you aspire to do. Not bad for a random picture in the flow of images in a photographer's life.

The thing that drives the content of the pictures are the same that drive the creator (photographer) of these pictures. We don't know why it is like that, but there seems to be a slight chance that the evolving ideas when you make a breakthrough in your creating brings on a flood of creativity. Maybe it is about that you become sure of what you are doing and thus are able to create yet additional "good" images. To that end it is not about the quantity, but about your own, inner voyage. Once you have started to fathom that there is a limit to the numbers of images you may create in your lifetime, you will probably want to push yourself a bit. At least aiming at making some of them manifest themselves in reality!

The process taking place when practicing is all about learning a craft. So, you have learnt a lot when you may be able to take a look back on the road you have travelled. You will be amazed over how much knowledge you have acquired over time. You do not have to worry about that, my mother used to state, time and time again: "Knowledge is no burden!" Of course she was right, it is lack of knowledge that may become a problem in the long run. With that lack we will have to rely on others and try to trust their level of expertise. If you are comfortable with what you do you may concentrate on just creating your images.

If it is possible for you to take those giant steps forward, meaning that you leave the technical requisites aside (as you now know them by heart) and can focus on composing your pictures, you are much better off. You no longer have to get caught up in the middle of thinking about your tools every time you go for a shoot. You can return to the technical aspects when you are looking for a way of doing an image in another manner. Sometimes you will get surprised by the results you are able to bring home. At other times you will be filled with discontent. You will at times experience being proud over what you have managed to accomplish. That is no small thing.

Your way of working

The manner you go about learning new things might be an indication of how you work as a photographer. That is really all about what kind of person you are. Three obvious traits to deciding what kind of photographer are is one description of you is:

- I must try that, right away.
- I read the manual before I try to do anything.
- I experiment a lot, then I go make pictures.

Your aim is to incorporate all of the descriptions above in the way you handle your photography. It is okay to be eager to try things out, but read the manual of your camera first and, most important of all three is that you have to experiment with your camera and your photography. Try it all, then make your informed choice!

You might realize that you are a mix of the three photographers describe above. There is no need to worry about that, the chance is that you are a complex person. You have to remember that there is no right or wrong way or manner to make pictures. The main thing is to remember to have fun when you are making images. You will grow as a photographer each day even with tiny steps or seemingly no steps forward at all. Trust the learning curve! You will get there! Never forget that you will gain knowledge and insights if you have set your mind on loading your pictures with stories. In the long run you might even have made so many sets of pictures with some kind of stories that they could result in an exhibition, or a book. The sky is always the limit!

The pictures that you create are the children of your imagination. So, be kind to them, give them the best upbringing you are able to. Think about your images as traits of the past, bringing you into the future!

The results emanating from you practicing the art of photography; experimenting and speculating on your way to better photography is in a manner of speaking a method to let your photography grew better. Practicing will help you gain self-assurance and 'cockiness' in a way you never experienced before. If it is good or bad is for you to decide. If you feel confident that everything is going well, but you have a hunch that the results do not 'feel' like you, keep on in the tracks for a while, and if that feeling of uncertainty still lingers, make a reboot! Try something else. Life is too short for us to wrestle with methods that do not work for us. Let others try them!

Try something new! Or, if you are determined to become a 'great artist' you might have to struggle through the rough parts of your apprenticeship in order to gain knowledge and confidence to dare venture into the world. You might have to 'suffer' a bit to get there. That means you will have to endure a lot of boring exercises, some tedious repetitions of stuff you are convinced that you already have a grip on. Assuming that you make your living doing other things than photography it means that you do not have that much time to spend making pictures. You should not worry too much about hard suffering either. It does mean, however, that you have to feel somewhat uncomfortable at times, at least until you have picked up some new tricks of the trade. But, don't put up with a feeling of discomfort that lingers on for months and months on time. That state of mind is not good for anyone. It is important that you feel good about yourself and what you are doing. Try not to worry about stuff that is of no importance. You want to do great pictures and do not want to worry about the way things generally are taught in the trade.

So, let us assume that everything will work out for you with the new things you have picked up and paired with the new ambitions you have acquired. As a result your pictures are becoming more interesting over time and you are rather content with the new things that you have taught yourself. Now, this is a good point in time – you might have become so good at making photographs that you may sketch what you want to realize in a photograph at home at your kitchen table. That is the moment when you start off planning your *Big Picture Project*. You might for example sketch lines and angles you want to incorporate into your future picture, you might sketch shadows that would be interesting to experience in real life. Then go out hunting for the elements of your sketches. Compose pictures and expose them, go out again and yet again. Try to load the pictures with more of a story than before. At first it will look like you are shooting the same, boring pictures time after time. But do not worry, this is like drills for an athlete. In athletics you cannot use full force until you have learnt the proper way to perform a movement. Regard your repeated shooting of approximately the same scenes time after time as the technical drills of an athlete. Bring your pictures home and go through them, then the tedious fixation of making what seems like the identical picture repeatedly will force you to shoot variations of the motifs, otherwise you will go mad.

The way you cope with the stream of pictures coming out of your change of method will decide how well you will adjust to your new insights. If you are no friend of stress, continue the way you are used to, don't change a thing, you don't want to become a nervous wreck practicing a hobby. If you can stand the stress that change will inflict upon you, go for it! It will not be the end of the world if you don't pull through, but think about how sad you will be in the future if you never tried to better your photography. As always, if you never try you will never find out if you have what it takes. There is nothing more depressing than people of mature age telling me: "I was photo-chum with John Doe (well-known photographer) when we were in our twenties, but then he made that exhibition and got famous and I lost my interest." Imagine! Now, everything works out well for your former friend and you can probably not take that and just congratulate him!

Never look back! And never compare your own work in any disadvantageous way with other people's work. What you did or didn't do yesterday or twenty years ago cannot be altered, but you still can do that thing now. Do not fret over that 'everybody else' may have done it already ten years ago. You didn't, so for you it is a novel experience. It is a risky business to look too much at what others do or don't do, you may lose focus on what you yourself ought to be doing. That is a thought that holds to measure for a whole lot of other things than photography. Keep your own photography at the center of your thoughts, nobody else's photography. During the time it takes to become better at what you do you have to practice. Don't practice only the stuff you are good at; you know how good you are at that. It's all the other things that you have an interest in becoming more proficient at that are at stake here. Those areas may need a lot of practice. When you are making photography you are training your eyes to 'see' things in a new manner in the surrounding world.

Your equipment is just a set of tools, on the same level as an axe or a guitar. You can do a whole lot of different things with those tools, but they are not crucial for your final result. You need a tool (camera) to make pictures in a photographic manner, but that tool does not create any pictures.

You might be a believer of tools of the latest technology, but don't buy equipment that means that your kids will not get the clothes and shoes they need. In other words, work towards gathering a set of equipment that you can afford in a realistic sense, not in a fantasy kind of world that you really are not a part of. Speaking of unrealistic, this is a manner of changing the world, producing great pictures – relaying your innermost thought into image files on a hard drive. You must try to convert your ideas, dreams or thoughts into some kind of reality, that is, into those image files. That is the hard, and only way, to visualize or convert, your ideas with all their connotations, reworking and influencing into the package you are trying to deliver. You may try your way around the infinite possibilities and make your own selection and try to show it to the world. Possibly people will recognize what you are trying to do, since no man is an island, but deeply connected into the surrounding culture, or maybe rather the culture we grew up within. Of course you will have picked up influences from other cultural groups on the way towards being the person you are today. We constantly pick up things as our lives go on. Even the use of languages other than our first language, will help us pick up new concepts. We might not be aware of what we have picked it up, until years later when we watch a movie and recognize arguments in it from a book we read twenty years ago. That is some kind of luggage we carry with us during our lives and it will become inseparable from what we are. It will become a part of us.

Some of it we will incorporate, other things we just skip over and go on looking for other things to use as influence. That is the baggage we carry on forever in our lives after the initial contact, that baggage will aid us interpreting our environment and it helps us decide whether we understand or just are baffled or frightened by things we experience.

Everything we have gone through in our lives remains in our output of images. It is a complex and rather interesting process that never stops to have us undergo changes of attitude. What we once thought was a good picture might have changed into something below par, when we take a look at it a couple of months later. What does that imply? We, as individuals seem to be the same, but that is far from true. We are constantly developing.

Don't even bother trying to understand why it is like that, even if you manage to do some shots it has to do with that the camera is considered being a "machine" making images, while other visual artist may use tools like charcoal, pencils or brushes to create their images. Since those artists are looked upon as more 'skilled' and their output will automatically be considered to be worth much more than a photographic image. The camera has been looked upon as the tool that, in a way, "industrializes" the making of images. Nowadays, in the digital era even more so.

Don't let that bother you when you have chosen photography as your means of expression. You don't make the rules that everyone else should have to follow. You might even ask yourself if it's that important what others categorize your photographs as being. You create your pictures because you can, and want to. That is all there is to it.

Yes, you might get some boosting of your ego when posting pictures on social media like Facebook and/or Instagram. The risk is that you will get a lot of likes. Remember that likes in any group, in social media or in real life, really only indicate that you struck the mother lode of mainstream in that group. It does not necessarily mean that your pictures are objectively good (if there exist something like objectivity). What it means is that your pictures are close to the mainstream ideas of what constitutes "a good image" in that group, amongst friends or other social settings. Your pictures do not have to be considered good anywhere else. You are only representing the mainstream taste and/or ideas in the setting you get praised in. That means that you should not put too much value on that praise, you might deceive yourself. What you ought to do is discuss your pictures with people that are not sitting on their high horses with a rigid view on what constitutes "a good picture". They are more prone to be honest. They will not try to convince you that you are a bad-ass photographer, when you internally feel that the truth is that you are not.

Discuss your images with people whose knowledge you respect. They are preferably not too drenched in mainstream concepts of what constitutes a "good" picture. A picture might be technically without flaws, but if it is totally void of any content whatsoever, there is no chance anyone will praise it. So, you might say that I support content free from technical mumbo-jumbo. The work that in my opinion turns out to be the most interesting is free from all "exoticism" or artsy stuff that will get praised at art galleries and museums just because it is made in a faraway place on earth. If you could wrap all that into an image made on your own backyard, it would be so much more interesting, since that indicates that the photographer has begun to really see (and presumedly to convey stuff).

If you are the kind of person who wants to think of creating some kind of new angle on photography you will have a lot to do. The pictures that will spread your emotions among other people will demand a different "loading" of the pictures with more than the diagonals, the "exotic" locations in the picture or, the (for you) "exotic" individuals you caught in your frame. The limit is already reached and no more work can be done in that area.

It's with restrictions that grow more and more narrow that you will hone your skills to perfection. Practice and limitations are the true foundation of great photography. Imagine that you decide to have "sky" in every picture you do during a month. After a couple of weeks you are looking for a chance to step out of that boundary and NOT include "sky", but persist for a while longer with your ambitions. You will reach borderline cases that demand so much more attention than the "sky" pictures. You will soon become adept at including "sky" into your work, and you will start longing for something more, something more complex. That means that you are well under way.

It's all about trying to expand your proficiency, making the pictures you envision, rather that settle for the pictures you manage to capture. The efforts you make are all for you and you increasing skills. Don't think of this work as a part of the road to success or, becoming influential among your peers. If things like that is going to happen, given the circumstances of your life, it will happen, but it might also be the case it does not ever occur. You will still practice a rewarding hobby. You will be getting better and better making your pictures as the first year passes. The obstacle you face is that almost all your peers are also improving, given that they invest equal amounts of time and effort as you do. You are not able to stop them from improving, so you either have to practice very much more, or stop comparing yourself with certain individuals. One idea is even to narrow the topic down to "pictures of dogs" or whatever is your favorites. Go all in with a specific photographic object and try to improve doing only that. Go for improving a lot! You have to admit that there is a lot of undeveloped talent around you and when those individuals go for it, they threaten to outgrow you in a big way. Beware of all the gifted people that seem to be born with a keen eye and a fast-moving intellect to back up their talent.

If you don't happen to be one of those persons with great talent, you have to try at least twice as hard. Some are born with an amount of talent; others have acquired skills in other fields like the arts or in the graphic industry. They have practiced a lot and thus trained their minds to "see" pictures in a more profound manner. Once you have acquired those skills the "talented" ones no longer have any "advantage" over you. Now you are in sync with the world of the talented. After that it is all about practicing, trying and trying again and again. That is the rough design of how to get where you want to be.

What is the most important thing about photography? Some would say: a camera but others would insist that it is the photographer. I lean towards the latter. Anyone can buy a camera, but not all of them are able to make photographic images that engage the spectator in the act, not just the persons in the photo, relatives and close friends. To reach out to the outer sphere of viewers you must have something to say, i.e., your photographs must contain a story. That means that you can't just make pictures where we recognize your next of kin, and they recognize themselves. You have to do better than that, you have to make it far better than the thought you have that these pictures are nicely exposed and composed. The people in the pictures might be nicely placed in the pictures and the lighting might be good, but there is something lacking. You have to put these questions to yourself: do these pictures tell a story about my family, or are they only some pictures of my family members? It is, of course, okay to make photos of your relatives, but to reach out to others, outside your family, and get them interested in those pictures, you have to create that story. How you manage that is up to you, but here are a few pointers:

1. Make images where people gaze at each other, and/or into the camera.

2. Aim at pictures with interaction between the figures in it, see above about gazes.
3. Use all kinds of paraphernalia; balls, computers, badminton racket. i.e. gadgets that add to the story you are trying to tell.

If grandpa is writing a book about his ancestors, place him at his desk busy doing just that. If your grandchild is playing soccer, see to it that she is busy with a ball. You get my drift? Show what people are interested in to start telling stories about them.

Stories are, as I have stressed several times earlier in this book, the bread and butter in creating compelling photographs. If you start with your family and the pictures you make of them you can build on that and building more interesting images of your relatives by, for examples, letting your relatives bring stuff relating to their hobbies or professions to the shoot you do with them. That is a good start to learning how to pack your images with stories. As time passes you might lighten up on the props; you don't have to be too obvious and have all the stuff in the picture. Your pictures will probably be better if future spectators have to think about your picture to crack the story. It is fine if you are able to add even more, you might get your husband to bring grandpa some refreshments, while grandpa is working on his book. Even better if your husband happens to be a professional waiter and can wear his uniform. You get my drift? The more threads you can weave together, the tighter and more comprehensive your story will become. Of course you might even try to use one of the blessings of digital photography – its low price – and horse around, making hundreds of frames really playing with your pictures. Remember that not even your relatives will play along forever, so one advice is to write down some ideas just in case your ideas on location are not flowing that easy

You may have fun while you are shooting your relatives and if you are lucky you might have stories built into your pictures as you go along. One test you might conduct is to show some pictures to persons not being your relatives. I stress that SOME pictures, don't strain your friendship with people. If some crumbles of stories are detected by your friends, you are on your way.

You might try taking notes while you are experimenting with images and producing them. If you are the more planning type you might create folders on your computer for those pictures you want to experiment further on with the help of image manipulation software. You might have special idea of what is possible to do with certain images, so save them for later. You have the possibility to duplicate the folders, try some filters or manipulation on copies, never the original file. Having specific copies manipulated in different manners give you the possibility to compare your different approaches. In this way you will learn what the filters of your software really does with your image files. You might also type up ideas in your word processor and leave those files in your folders. Those files might contain ideas, reflections or reminders for your future work. This is a manner of becoming your own teacher, and in a way start grading your own work, based on your old knowledge, and hopefully supplemented with your recent insights.

You will find that over time you will have a lot of use of these folders during your experimenting exercises. You ought to check in on them from time to time. After a couple of months you will see improvement. Your pictures will gradually become more interesting and more professional looking. The idea is to keep a journal over what you do and how you treat your images, checking every deviation from the process you started out using. This will of great help during your further development. You will be able to note even small, presumably significant, but vague, advances in your handling of your picture content. Over time you might even begin to notice that you are becoming even more comfortable when applying the new ideas and concepts you have developed as you move along. That will make you feel good about your work and that is a major thing to value. You do not want to keep at a hobby that makes you feel miserable. Be sure to note that you are becoming more seasoned and confident. You might even come up with ways of using your camera that you haven't thought of earlier. This might render a feather in your hat.

The images you produce will work as some kind of diary. The images will come out of your head and land in your computer in a manner that you, and only you, have any control over. It's all about getting these two aspects of imagery. You encounter reality, which is your raw material for producing your pictures. During that encounter you make a series go decisions that will decide what picture you decide is yours. Looking at your outcome, your "finished" images, you might want to start all over with them or new ones on the same themes. If you are able to stick it out while doing that time and time again, you are getting somewhere.

Becoming a "better photographer" might even mean that you evolve into a different kind of photographer than you are when you started out developing your skills methodically, trying to develop your skills. As stated earlier, it might mean that you will end up making a whole new kind of pictures. You might find that you really wanted to become a totally different kind of photographer than you thought you only could dream of becoming. You might develop a knack for making pictures of dogs and cats, or sports, and end up stopping to pursue the kind of motifs you used to concentrate on. You may continue to shoot street photography or musical events, but your main interest has suddenly a different focus. Don't you fret, it is still you making the new pictures!

You are, as an amateur, totally free to experiment making your images. When you deliver pictures on assignment you cannot experiment with the whole cluster of images. A pro is expected to deliver the basic pictures that were agreed on, not something completely different. You may deliver some more experimental images as a bonus. Like when you are making pictures for real estate agencies, they have a set of specifications on how you are supposed to deliver your images. You can use novel ideas, but they are outside your assignment which is usually very standardized.

In this part some things like using the natural settings and the wardrobe, like your uncle being a police officer may have his uniform on during the photo-shoot with him, has been discussed.

The main feature discussed above is:

- practice the stuff you're bad at, since that the parts of your skills that you have to get up to par

Less is more

Above I have presented a bunch of ideas on how to make your pictures more complex and in a manner, telling more of a story. They will then become more interesting for others outside your family or your ring of fellow photography aficionados. This will offer the random viewer to sense somewhat welcomed into the realm of your images are describing. In a way this an adaptation of the old saying that; "less is more". What that means, at least here and now, is that you have to simplify your pictures. You might start with missions like "human shot from behind in bad lighting". There are a lot of options for a shot like that, some of them will render the figure almost as a silhouette. Another option is to step in closer so that you, being the first viewer, catch a glimpse of something in this set-up. That means that you can shot the back, the neck or the feet of the person in front of you. All those shots have the capacity to become images. They might be fractions of the world around you, but they obviously, still will be your interpretation of the world around you.

"Less is more" may also refer to colors, keep them in a strict leash and you will achieve a certain "look" in your pictures. You may even try out creating collections of pictures where a certain shade of a color appears in all the pictures in your collection. It may be achieved by cloning a color and substitute accents of your entire collection in your image processing software. Some people regard this as cheating, adding or substituting colors, but as long as you don't argue that your picture is a documentary image, you'll be fine. If you check out books and magazines, you will find that certain articles may be designed with the help of color accents, some of them "natural", some of them not so much. It may keep the article together though, so as a means of accomplishing that, it is not uncommon in the media. Some brands advertised really are dependent on color hues, if missed risking to overthrow the entire concept of that brand. You will be wise not to overdo it, though.

Try out the ideas you have about color. Make, for example, pictures containing blue elements, but do not use the sky, please! You may choose any color you want just for this exercise of making about a dozen pictures with a common color denominator and incorporate your chosen color hue on them. They will appear to be more alike when they get that dot of the same color hue. Then you could also test photographing series of stuff like doors, lampposts, neon signs, door handles or trash cans. You will probably come up with loads of new ideas – but making some series of pictures of stuff that a viewer will recognize, like, let us say bicycles. Look at what you are able to do with motifs like that. You have to dig deep down into your fantasy to create something like that.

Strange things might happen when you go out looking for some theme to shoot. If you did not reflect over you themes beforehand, you will now cease to reflect and you will discover ladies in pink, or guys with neck tattoos. Once you have spotted one of the subjects, always the same theme, others will emerge right in front of you in the street from time to time. It will go on and on, even years after you did your first shoot within a theme. When we teach ourselves to observe, really scanning our surroundings, it seems we cannot reverse that knowledge acquired. We will gaze at people and things with what some cop friend called the "cop gaze". That gaze is too long, some will get disturbed when you're looking at them in this manner.

According to my friend cops tend to stare a bit longer than ordinary people usually do when we meet the eyes of other people. In real terms it is not that long, a fraction of a second, perhaps. It is longer though than the gazes from the ordinary passersby and we notice that. My friend further stated that there are two other kinds of people that break that minimal time frame in the same manner as cops do. The two other groups of people are psychopaths and drug addicts on a high. So, don't get surprised if you receive funny stares back when you look around, or that they appear to be angry. There is no doubt that they have spotted you!

There are a lot of games that will help you along your path to becoming a better and a more interesting photographer. But, again, no one is going to do your work for you, so you have to get out there starting to track down targets and do things when you conduct your shooting. The world was essentially created, it has been said, to be photographed. Thinking along that line photography might sometimes be a spiritual endeavor. Not so much a religious, but rather a spiritual journey. You go out there into the world and you will return home with some pictures to show for your trip. Some would argue that those images are of the world in the same sense that the hunter's prey is. Photography has a lot to do with hunting.

You may not catch the prey that you desire the most every time you are out, but you might catch some specimen that will do for now. Like sometimes you maybe want to put some trophies on your wall? The dos or don'ts are yours to decide. Maybe you want to live in a cocoon with your own pictures surrounding you, or maybe not? There are pros and cons with that way of handling your pictures. You possibly want to see them from time to time, okay!

Beware of that the effect that pictures hanging on your walls will disappear during your everyday routines. They are still hanging there on your walls, but you cease noticing them since your mind is aware that you already have noticed them. Your brain usually works very efficiently and does not do the same amount of work twice. But when you might be tired you might experience something in a *déjà vu* experience. Or rather a reversed *déjà vu*, when you rediscover your pictures on your walls, surprised at first but later arriving at the insight that they have been hanging there all the time.

Maybe you should create routines for how you study your own pictures? If you do it when studying others, why not systematize your 'self-studies' too? You could try to expose yourself to some pictures that you print it in 20x30 cm and let them lie loose in a cardboard box. Now and then you leaf through that pile of pictures and ponder over them. "What was I trying to capture here, what was I trying to express here, what does this image tell me now, when I have half forgotten how it was created"? You might want to write down your ideas about what to try for.

One idea, speaking about pictures in your home, is to make pictures of stuff in your home. No people, no selfies, just the stuff you have gathered and making that tell the story about you. Every picture should contain some part of the story about you. The full story, told by your home, will reveal itself when someone studies all of the pictures you present, made in your home. Every picture tells a part, and together the set of images will tell the complete story about you and your home.

Try this as an exercise, and threw in some frames where you try to mimic the style of real estate photography, like you were going to sell your home. Minimalism is the key in real estate photography these days. The images have to show what potential your home has in becoming someone else's home.

You will practice a kind of photography most people have ever never considered. There might be some new insights to learn from that exercise! There is a lot of thinking about practice and exercises in this text. My thought behind this is that I think that if we call them exercises and practice it will take the edge out of the photo shooting. To bring a playful feeling when you create your pictures might help you to relax and really "see" the possibilities of every motif. In that way you will not be "working" but rather fool around playing which will help you relax a bit. This will mean a lot of difference between these two manners of working; one being very serious, and the other more based on play. Perhaps it is possible to mix those two ways of develop your own photography. They will probably mix and propel you into a new sphere of photography. In that new realm you will probably grow a new attitude, or at least refresh your existing attitude, towards your own photography. That must be a good thing. In a way we are *homo ludens* (the playing man) and we like playing, and sometimes our playing will result in a lot of work being done. At times the two aspects of photography will unite into only one. They will become so intertwined that it will be impossible so see where the borders between them are – if there even are borders between them after a while. The borders might disappear in the sessions of playful photography you can devote yourself to make.

In this part some things like how you handle your projects have been discussed. Some of the main features discussed above are:

- write down your ideas about what to try for
- create folders for your projects
- revise your project from time to time as they develop

Chaos Photography

You might even venture to try some "chaos photography". Since the world around us is constantly changing, go with it. Aim boldly, shoot recklessly and watch what comes out of the session. What we are looking for is fast decision making, fast aiming and fast shooting. Think of yourself as a wild west gunslinger stereotype. If it moves, shoot. If it catches your eye, shoot! During a session like this one hour should at least render 60 DIFFERENT images. That means that you will discover, aim and shoot every minute, and the next minute and so on! This will train you to get ready for the shot rapidly and not to discard ideas before you have tried them out. You will probably find that in the beginning you do not make any pictures that you want to call good, but wait for it, you will become so much faster and more secure in your aiming that you don't have to think about your equipment when you are out there. After a few sessions of this regime you will find that you don't nibble around as much, shoot faster, more accurately and – best of all – you don't miss out on so many opportunities!

In contrast to chaos photography you could restrain yourself to looking for one frame every 15 minutes. That will mean that you bring home four frames per hour. Compare that result to the one you got when you practiced chaos-photography – now you have four meticulously chosen frames in your camera. Did you learn anything practicing these so totally different manners of approaching the world you want to makes pictures of and about?

Hope you did. You might even break it down to even smaller pieces as building blocks in order to be sure that you conquer them one at a time. Few of us have the capacity to work in many genres at the same time and become good all over. It is good to know a little of everything – after all, it's all photography – you don't need to become a complete jack of all trades – that would mean that you're a decent craftsman in all aspects of photography, but not especially good at anything. So, rather than working to cover all aspects of photography most of us have to niche ourselves.

To really become excellent at one kind of photography is a big task, so as time goes by, try to narrow your "major" field of photography down. It is fun to shoot everywhere and anything, some shots work in several field of photography. You have to look upon the majority of your photographic endeavors as "limbering up" for your main work within the photographic field. A sprinter in track and field, for example, might dabble in a lot of events during off-season, but has as a rule only one side specialty, often the long jump. A shot putter might double in discus. The reason for the one-sided work with one event or one aspect (like in photography) is that it takes time and considerable effort to become good. It takes a lot more time and effort to stay that good. Since track & field events are based mostly on physical skills you cannot peak for many years.

Photography, on the other hand, really is not primary physical, even if making loads of pictures in extreme heat or cold, or, at high altitudes, or way out in the wilderness, is not for everyone. Other kinds of photography may really be for everyone — it is possible to specialize so far off the mainstream photography that it is doable. You might find yourself so far away that you might end up being the only one bringing your photo gear to that neighborhood.

What do I really argue here? The answer is; specialize, but only to a certain extent. You do not want to become so specialized that you enable your capacity to make photographs in all genres. You really want to be able to make photos in any genre — but you do not want to have to travel to certain places, wait for a certain season or plan meetings with certain people to be able to continue shooting your kind of material. To keep your photography alive you must in some sense stay an omnivore, alternatively with a taste for something special.

This may appear to be more complicated than it really is. You concentrate on one kind of photography, but your skills are constantly being tested as you make pictures continuously, even within other genres. It is that simple and it is very easily done. You may as a side project have some tedious idea like making a picture of your house from the same spot on the sidewalk every day. You might make that photo in the morning or when you return home. You might even make an image of what you eat for breakfast every day during a year. After a year you will have a story to present!

Be childish! Simple ideas have a magnificent power, and if you do not have to arrange what you shoot, it will be done. You will even find your targets in what other people do. Starting to look around in your own life you will discover that other people present their lives for you to shoot and save until it is time to present the hundreds of pictures you have made of their lives. Will they buy your images as a memory of what they have done, as a way of assuring you that your pictures are good, or for some other reason? Does it mean that there is a commercial aspect to what you are doing? Mind you, that is not so important.

It might be a new experience discovering how fast you can sell a picture! Let me remind you that selling to friends, or private individuals over all, will not create the income you might need to allow your photography to stand alone, economically, that is! That kind of selling will never get you rich and/or famous, if that is something you aspire to become. It is nice that someone will pay a handful of dollars for an image. One way to increase that income is to sell via photography brokers on the Internet. They charge a commission, but remember that you probably would not sell pictures at all if you have no connections to companies that need images of your kind. Selling pictures via an image broker is like having someone working for you and taking care of delivering and billing at the same time. So, you may be free to be out there, making a lot of new impressive images. You don't want to get caught up in bureaucracy, or other time-consuming tasks.

Another way of creating revenue is to produce your own photo-books with a company dealing with print-on-demand-services. Once you have uploaded your PDF-files you don't have any hassle with handling the books and see to it that they are mailed to the people eager to purchase them. It is all taken care of within the contract you have with the POD-agent on the Internet. You may make more pictures and create yet other books. You may order your own books well below the retail price and use them at exhibitions, or, when you are asked to speak about photography and so on. It is a risky business so don't bring home more books than you can sell in six months. Your money is locked up in the books you bring home. It is so very easily done to overestimate the interest in your books.

As you probably understand by now, there are several ways to reach out with your images.

One underestimated role is played by your blog or a web site of some kind. Start with a free one, like Blogger and put some of your pictures there. Decide if you are going to write supporting texts for your images or not. You might want some text in every post, since the probability that you picture will show up in a search on Internet will then increase. Of course the traffic to your blog will increase if you do updates once in a while. It is a sad thing finding something of interest on the web, navigating to that spot and check the dateline and discover that it has not been updated in seven years! You wonder whatever happened.

In general, there is a lot of work needed to reach

out, way ahead of people that you call friends or acquaintances, to reach others that are willing to pay some bucks to see more of your pictures. It is possible to make that happen if you constantly update your digital portfolio, whatever the shape, and it seems obvious that you still are working on it.

Some wise guy once wrote: "You can eat an elephant; it's just about chewing away 200 grammes of elephant each day and soon the elephant will be gone!". That is really as valid for other things in life. One step at a time and you will reach your goals. The key thing is to keep on going, not always at the same pace, but one foot before the other, all of the time.

I figure that this is one way with everything we learn and try to become increasingly more skilled at doing, constantly growing more experienced. Our interests sometimes will take leaps into directions we will be surprised to realize. These leaps will sometimes interest us for a while, then that sudden interest will fade away. But, be sure that they are still lingering somewhere in your subconscious and suddenly they will pop out again, when you least expect them to do it. Since we only have a certain amount of energy it sometimes might seem like too much, but do not worry. You might in spite of this engage in plans that span over several years when you figure you should have met with a lot of stuff you are not familiar with, and do not even want to bother with.

That is a good thing — to look ahead, but always be aware that everything you want to learn will take time. Some skills will take forever and others, possibly not skills, but more of short cuts or tricks of the trade, will not take that long to try out, then reject or keep within your own tool box. Time is a resource that is sparse and have to be snatched from other parts of your life for you to be able to learning new things.

In this part some of the main features discussed are:
• Don't discard images before you try to shoot them.
• Don't go only with what you want to do, be bold, and shoot anything.

Commitment

I do not want to advise you to chance all your luck on photography forsaking all other pleasures in life. When I read what I have written in the previous pages it looks like I am trying to set up rules for some kind of warrior monk of photography with a lot a practice drills and talk about always being prepared, like a boy scout or a soldier. This is just one extreme end of this hobby called photography. We have to be honest about that it might be any day out making pictures, then back feeding the images into the image processing software of your choice, that will reveal that awesome image we have constantly been chasing for.

I know that as an amateur photographer (a person that does not make his living by photography) you have to make room for other important things in your life such as family and friends other than the photo buffs you probably hang out with on a regular basis. You have to live an ordinary life in order to not get dependent on photography for a living. Enjoy life, make photographs and have a ball!

But, remember to bring your camera all the time. You might discover images energizing even in the paths of your life that you usually do not connect with your photography. One way of thinking about it is this; since light is a natural phenomenon that makes it possible to create images at all, and light is everywhere, making it possible to create pictures anywhere at any time. The picture making does not have to take much time away from what you primarily are at the location to do. Be aware that your employer might not like you taking too many pictures as he is paying you to occupy yourself with something else. If you are "good with people" you might "happen" to catch some really good frames spontaneously among your regular friends. Note that when they get accustomed to you having a camera with you at all times, and "always" is using it, you are on your way to become the "chronicler" of your friends' lives.

You will be there with your camera until they count on you being there with your camera. They will miss you when they don't hear your shutter rattling, so there are no excuses! You understand that I presuppose that you will be making photos everywhere, even if I think that it is a good thing to narrow your goals down, and specialize. The time you don't make pictures you have to earn a living, spend time with your family, etc. Generally, taking some time off from photography is a good thing if it is a part of you master plan and you are the master of your schedule. A fortnight without camera will make you more 'hungry' to start again. Don't let too long a time lapse before you reconnect with your camera again. One idea is to relax with your photography and take classes in sketching to improve your ability to "see" and understand images. It will often be both time and money wisely spent.

It might even make you more ambitious and things you pick up during sketching class might influence the manner in which you make your photographic images. You might even learn to understand what an image is and how it works, without your camera. Then it is about time to apply it to your work with your camera in hand.The insights you gain are a way to let you understand more of light versus less light and it helps you create an image in any which light.

You will have to live with being "the person with the camera". As time passes your camera will become a part of your persona to the degree that you will feel awkwardly naked without it. That is the way a tool well used will work, it will in time become a part of you, of who you are, being the person that is able to do things with this tool that you cannot do without it. Since a lot of cameras in this digital era are, in a manner of speaking, developing us into some kind of cyborgs, with the camera always in your hand will make the device a part of you.It will help you catch what you see, consciously or subconsciously. Your brain will do that too, but the problem with the brain is that it cannot print those images (unless you are a superb sketching artist). The brain is poor to process your images in the manner that is possible with image processing software.

Sometimes you may ask yourself: Which is the most interesting photograph you have ever seen? What genre would you say it belongs in? What about trying to copy pictures like that as an exercise? The elements in the pictures you make do not have to be exactly the same, but what you have to get right is the important basic structure of the image. That is, the core structure, like perspective and the location of major element in the picture have to be recognizable. You must put emphasis on the effects of the light and the relation between the major components in the image you are creating. Think of it as learning a new language. You have to get the basic sounds reasonably right, then a minor accent is okay.

You do not have to go to war in order to copy the structure of a picture from a war scene. Like, you do not have to travel to Bhutan to use the image structure in a picture from a minor village square. You have to learn and understand the inherent structure of these images. Of course, you are not supposed to use this formula every day and with every picture you do. The idea is to train your eye to compose the picture in the camera so you do not have to process the image with a lot of cropping. You can do all that while being in the field. I argue that the relationships between the elements in the picture is what creates the "story" hidden in the picture. The earlier experiences of the viewer adding on to that, to create a 'story'.

This is the idea: you compose a picture containing the elements in front of you – shifting camera angles, focal point and zooming in or out to crop the image from where you are standing, or taking a few steps either backwards, forwards or to either side to reach the desired result. Old school art schools had their students spending a lot of time copying the "old masters" obtaining a link between the eyes and the hand drawing the picture. That is also what this exercise is about. The hand is your camera and the eyes contains your gaze. The hand and the eyes must work together with your brain to decide when you are going to press the button. Remember that the camera is a tool and that it is possible to do anything with it in action every time you aim at a target. Trying to capture that moment, but somehow tainting it with your ideas is the aim of this exercise.

The idea that we might "save moments" from our lives and look at them later really is a mind boggling concept. In its small way it is like making some kind of copies of history in order to be able to study them in detail later on. It's like having a scrap book of the past to be readily looked at any moment you choose in the future.

Having the ability to "save" history or at least part of your own life is a remarkable power. It means that 10 years into the future we could look at the identical picture and marvel over how life was today. We are not to be surprised when we discover that the possibly ordinary events, that we lived through during the day the images were made and that means that we are in a situation where we are in some respect gone ourselves and recover this piece of history as some kind of gift. We know that printing an image will transform it into an object that will do well as a gift.

All things photographed don't have to have a body, an image is a thing even if it stored digitally on a memory card. It puts demands on space and that might be said about all documents that are stored digitally. In short, the images don't have to be placed on a wall. They still exist and may be talked about in all media, not only the digital ones.

We have to make a difference between images that have been printed and pictures that are dwelling within digital storage media. The question is if they are possible to compare. Isn't it a bit spooky that literally thousands of images may be stored on a memory card? Maybe it is just me, born too long ago and experienced by the shift from analog photography to digital? It might even be like that the images add up to something new just because they might be so many. The question is when we will learn to accept digital images on the same level as the analog ones.

They are not necessarily all good, but they are digital and they hide on hard drives, external back up facilities existing in "the digital cloud", and what not. You might discover that you have access to ten copies of the same image. Since you do your backups at fairly regular intervals always have the "master folder" intact in, at least, two secure locations, but that indicates that there are, in this case eight copies that are processed in some manner, or are in for some processing to fit into a project of some kind. You have to use a consistent system to keep track of what you do with your images, otherwise the situation soon will become rather confusing as you might find yourself in a spot where you cannot locate the original, or, unprocessed "original" of your image.

We might try to be careful about how we save our material, but there will be mistakes all along the way. There will be way more mistakes made over time!

If you deny that you like making images more than necessary it is depending on your routines for your photography. Never think: "I won't be needing my camera this weekend!" You are wrong in so many ways and you know it. You always need your camera, what were you thinking?

Don't make a fuzz about it. Just bring your camera! You'll notice when people get irritated by your snapping images everywhere and all the time. Then they will tell you to bring it down a bit. So, play it by ear and you will be okay. Sometimes you might need a short break from making images. Take that when you feel like it. Too much of anything is not good, and too little of something isn't good either.

So, you have to balance your everyday life and your photography. There is more to life than photography, but who wants to take a chance? If you take the chance on that it is okay living without photography, it's all in your doing. Please, tell me if you survive!

Tell me how it feels to walk through life without a camera. At second thought; don't tell me! I prefer living without knowing. I don't care and I don't want to know. I really think that you guys make that stuff up to annoy me.

But, seriously; where were we? All right, we were talking about if it ever has existed a day in anybody's life when it had been better not bringing a camera. As I recall it there has never been and will never come a day when this comes true. If you really want to know, I actually think there once was one, and that day was my birthday way back. I was not fit enough to bring one, so it didn't really work out for me. I didn't make ONE picture that day, but it was only because they were not letting me do it.

So, seriously, think hard! What would be the only event when you wouldn't bring a camera? I have some notions what that would be about, what kind of event that would prevent you from bringing the camera to the site.

There might be shows, museums and possibly public transportation that you can't use your camera. You have better check what the regulations are in the country where you work.

Most of the time it's our own inhibitions that will stop us from doing what we want to do. There are no real laws or rules hindering us from doing what we want. Often, we just "suppose" that stuff isn't permitted, and leave the camera at home. You may not like the way I am going with this, but life generally isn't the clear cut way we usually imagine it.

If you could choose a moment that you would like to preserve forever, what moment would you choose, given that others would like to save a moment from your specific life, not from the general run of world history. When I think about moments that I would like to save, based on my life, there are some that qualify, but I'm not dead sure what specific moment I would choose.

Not that there are so many moments that I would like to save in an image, but rather that they will change in value when I choose one image before all the others.

Having had an image of me receiving a grant in

sixth grade, much to my surprise, would probably have changed the value I put on that moment in time.

Where in time would the photo have been shot; when I heard my name being called up or when I bowed and shook the headmaster's hand? I am sure that having any of these photos would have changed my memory of that moment. I would maybe be able to see what kind of clothes I wore that day. Historical and biographical presences will add details to our memories. I remember going through my parents 2 1/4 x 3 3/4 negatives from the 1950s a couple of years ago in search of details on how the environment looked where my kid sister and me grew up. Okay, I found out that, especially our mom, had learnt the lesson well about "taking one step closer". Her pictures are very well cropped already in the negatives. My father's pictures, on the other hand, show some areas in the background, like the cottage and the fence around it. He had put up the fence himself and made some adjustments to the cottage during the years. I found some pictures of me and my sister, dressed in adjusted clothes we had inherited from our cousins, with patches on them. Mind you, this was in the 1950s, and children's clothes were not designed like today. My sister and I appear like we were raised at some cottage in the woods around the year 1900. So, that was a lesson to be learnt. My parents apparently snapped images of their children, the cottage and almost nothing else. In the snapshots of the cottage, you may see other cottages in the background. Going through the pictures from my childhood, knowing full well that taking pictures was rather expensive in the 1950s, so the pictures were probably only of scenes that they thought were well worth saving. The things that mattered most were the cottage and the kids. I wish that my parents had made more shots of the surroundings. Even if they were not really interested, they could have thought a bit about me and my sister when we were getting older and got more interested in where we spent our childhood and how it looked like in black and white.

Our parents left us with some pictorial memories, and that is a good thing, even if there could have been more. What has been done cannot be undone, but in a way, I still carry with me some sorrow over the fact that my childhood mostly exists in my head in the form of memories and I gather that it doesn't seem like we were poor, like in my memories. As a child I probably had no idea of how to distinguish between the two extremes. There were some instances of some kind of trauma, like when I came down with scarlet fever and was hospitalized just before starting first grade. I like to have had some pictures from the life on the hospital ward with a bunch of 6 to 10 years old boys! In my memory the daily routine there was not so stiff as you might think when you see arranged images from hospitals from that period.

So, the pictures we don't have access to might seem like a problem to us. They're not possible to create in hindsight, they're in a way lost forever. That's why it is so important to save a lot of images from today with information on geographical whereabouts, data and that sort of thing. Even if it is hard to believe that my external hard drives and other storage media will be preserved after I pass on, it is still to some good that I tried to save my bit of our common heritage. I really tried to save something of all those "moments" I have experienced during my life time.

Even if a lot of images in the future will not be saved, the attempt is a good one and I wish for more people doing their outmost to saving their images, otherwise it will only remain the images made on commission that will be saved. That will preserve some parts of the past, but the only one belonging to a solid mainstream view on what the past was like. This is some kind of material that is "saved in the barns" by millions of photographers around the world.

In the same manner as e-mail and free-to-build websites some images will be lost forever in the great digital void. Maybe somebody will stumble on them some time in the future, but you cannot be sure of that, can you? The e-mails of free accounts will dry out and web-sites will dry out with the last post reading: "Last updated on March 23, 1999". Of course, if you pay for your account, they will no longer be accessible when your payments stop. There will be scarce with traces everywhere. Some are copied and stored like the project run by The Royal Library, Sweden (Kungliga biblioteket). The way the possibility to write history in a better and more conclusive manner seems to be about having huge storage capacities to save the digital documents of today – postponing the interpretation and use of the content unto posterity.

In this part some things like the saving of images have been discussed. One of the main features discussed above is:

- see to it that you do backups of your images

Making a photo-book

So, if you really want to save your photographs one method is to do books. They will rest at the National library and will continue to exist when the last sold copy has vanished from the market. Maybe not forever, but for a very long time. The production of photo-books is a good exercise in selectivity regarding what pictures are going into the book. Is it a book about transportation, about "the last persons" reading a book in public space, or a book about sports events, or theatrical events you have been doing pictures of? You might have tried to make a book about ideas or concepts that are very hard to put into images. This book might not fit into the categories above. Never mind. The selection of images to bundle in a book is never an easy one. Let's say you spent a month in a town you don't know very well and have made loads of images there. You might have come to understand why you're fascinated by this town – a book might be the way to express some of that fascination. I think that the narrower and tighter you can make the selection; the more clarity you have within the story you create – connecting all the images with each other in the selection for your book. You must strive after and hope for, a lean and tight message. Or, you might trust the reader's imagination and you go for a book without even you understanding it from the start.

You might even consider making "chapters", cutting up the book along certain themes you discover during your selection of the basic heap of images you start out with. This might point to the diversity within your book, but the themes will become even tighter compared to the case when you just bundle all the images without divisor chapters. This might indicate a certain deeper content than in the case where you just go with the rhythm of the images initially brought together to be weeded out into making the content of your book.

Designing your first book will probably leave you with an appetite to produce a whole series of books. You design them as booklets of 32 pages with staples in their spine, or more complicated productions with over 200 pages, in some pocket book design or, with hardcover binding. Whatever you choose, be sure to spend time on the selection of pictures. I'm sorry to be the one breaking the bad news to you: there are always a couple of images that don't fit in when you scrutinize your first selection! You will probably even be surprised by how faded and mainstream your images appear to be. Maybe you should try another or, alternative, way of treating them in your image processing application?

The more you leave out, the more your selection for your book will gain in quality. You will end up with a bundle of images that you have discarded, and that is really good for your book, and even for you, since you'll be leaving out a whole lot of images, you'll the creator of a *good* photography book. Thus you will have gained a laurel that will follow you forever. You might even cross out that line "do a photo book" on your bucket-list. Thus you may even concentrate even more on making awesome images from here on.

Since making pictures is the name of the game when I look at some selection of my older images, I feel an urge to return back out there and redo some of them, since I am a so much better photographer than I was 60 years ago or, even six months ago, am I not? Some days I am, and other days I really start doubting what I am doing. It's like working on a roller coaster, to say the least, all of the time. In a manner of speaking I am a better (or maybe just more experienced) photographer than I was 60 years ago. The problem is that I really don't make pictures from the same motifs anymore, or, if I do, I don't pay the same attention to the same spots in the picture that I did all those years ago. I'm striving to make images from pictures I make like the "postcard-view", sports, theatrical events, street photography, storefronts and "objets trouvé". I make an effort to execute some like in the street photography I've been committed to the last ten years. It's all about being fast and bold. I strive to execute all my pictures in that fast and bold mood. Sometimes I lose heart and begin thinking that all my images are looking just the same. This doesn't worry me for long, though. I just click the shutter in front of a lot of things and people I pass during the day. I seldom go out to make pictures, the camera tags along whatever I'm up to and the images are found along my route for the day. That means, among other things, that I don't have a lot of sunsets. I like to make pictures in foggy weather. So, there I might be out at night, or in the early morning, when I become aware of a foggy situation, get my gear together and rush away towards some place where there are people, traffic, roads crossing, or a bridge of some kind. That means that there are some fog images in my collections, together with a lot of sports photography, images from theatrical events, people I spot in the street, and so on.

When the images are captured and have landed in your computer, and you're leafing through them, there's one thing to remember well! Never delete images you've made before you've looked at them in full computer screen mode. If you check them out in the camera they might look all alike, but you will sometimes discover that you have been given "gifts" or "surprises" in the row of pictures when you check them out carefully. What seemed to be a rather boring image of a building's facade may have a person looking out a window in it. This turns this image into something totally different. Maybe not so good a picture if what you wanted in the first place was a human face, clean and crisp. As an everyday picture its use might be a good picture, or at least, a better picture than the ordinary architectural images I was going for at the moment.

So, an image might seem good in one aspect and appear not so good in yet another. The way we sort images into categories where they come alive is an interesting way of handling these saved memories of time. If we are too hard on ourselves, we cannot make our self-justice. So, play around with your images, sort them in different manners. Sort them into the "wrong" category and discover what happens with your appreciation of them! They might gain more life if they are juxtaposed to other images than you expected.

This book is printed and distributed via BOD.se, a company printing in Germany, but with an office in Sweden, where I live. You just upload your PDFs for the book's body and cover to the company's server, or you pay to have that done for you. Works great for me, but you might be in a different situation and will ponder the possibilities to scout for other options. People wanting my books may order them from an major Internet book dealer.

In this part some things like never deleting images until you have seen them in their full capacity on your computer screen, have been discussed. Some of the main features discussed above are:

- Making a photobook
- Go through your material, time, and time again.

Humour

Humor is a risky business. What I find funny isn't necessarily stuff that you will laugh at. My advice is to avoid "freak" shots, it is not a humanistic manner to present ordinary people in a bad way. The images might seem funny at the moment, but when you look at them later you might experience a rather sour taste in your mouth. Refrain from it, if is not funny in a delicate and compassionate manner. You don't want to do images where people are grotesque in your eyes or are made fun of in the eyes of the possible viewers. Pictures like that will still leave some very mixed-up ideas about your images and the content of them. Refrain from stuff like that! Someone might argue that we should make images of the world as we find it. Fine! Don't write captions that are demeaning and cruel to the figurants in your image.

When you experience down periods in your photography and don't make as many images as usual, have you ever thought about why that occurs? The *first reason* might be that it has been some time since you got enthusiastic over one of your more recent images, you're descending into your "creative mode". A *second reason* might be a lack of inspiration. You haven't seen enough images for a while, or even made too few of them. Leaf through photo books, scroll through relevant parts of Internet, or watch movies (there's really good camera work in a lot of them). I'll give you a *third reaso*n on why you're bored; maybe even overfed by too many pictures.

It might be good for you to slack off a bit, until you feel the urge to make awesome images again.

The way to nourish your interest for photography might at times be like any other type of learning and acquiring of skills. You happen to stagnate, or at least you figure that, it is no fun, even if you understand that the learning curve can't be forever steep. It has to even out the remaining bumps in your vision and is only allowing for minor additions to your knowledge as time goes by. Don't panic, you're doing fine, maybe you just need a treat, a refill of learning or knowledge, maybe even a switch to motifs you usually don't use that much?

When I was active within martial arts, we sometimes practiced to hone at least three ways out a situation during the fight. These three solutions depend, of course, on where you stood in relation to your opponent. Sometimes the fight went along so you might have to use all of your applicable techniques, one after the other. In a way, motifs come to you much alike the way an opponent goes at you. Try one way, then another, maybe you solve the situation in your third attempt, maybe you won't. The bottom line is that you should aim for more diversity within your range of ideas for pictures.

Even as a photographer it may be wise to obtain an arsenal of 'tricks' in order to land that big fish, the ultimate awesome picture. We'll skip the most obvious one – you have to bring your camera, preferably in your hand – and be out here, scouting for images.

A first suggestion is an idea with two sides. Either

you go looking for people to make pictures off – or you look for places that usually are filled with people and you set out to make loads of images of that place when it's totally void of people. The contrast will be effective. Maybe you have to present a before (with people) and an after without people picture to get the most out of it. I was thinking in terms of making a picture of an empty Japanese subway contrasting it to rush hour status. Maybe it must not be a risk that the picture will look arranged, but it's an idea to play around with, like presenting someone who is known to be always straight and stern and you succeed in presenting that person mildly laughing!

In order to suggest a *second technique* I think you should try shooting from the hip. It is controversial and a risky business since you're not exactly sure about the framing of the image will be. You may practice making selfies instead of full body versions. Then you'll learn that you have to tilt the camera to catch what you are seeing from the level your eyes are situated. There is quite a discrepancy between what you actually see and what your camera will catch. It will take some time and you will use up some of your battery's life, but that can be recharged, or replaced with one of your spare batteries, so this is no biggie! Practice so you'll become so accurate as to be able to decide if you're cutting off someone's head before you press the trigger. You might even practice with your camera in hand in front of a full body mirror, that you might have at home. Stand in front of the mirror, camera in hand, trying to aim it at the image of yourself in the mirror. Eventually you get the hang on how much you have to tilt the camera to get the picture you want. Then try it outside, shooting billboards, traffic signs and store-front windows. Mastering this manner of shooting will enable you to pass through a crowd of people and catch almost everyone without their noticing. No hassle, no discussions! Maybe the result will an image that is not particularly good, but those will come to you!

For a third suggestion I propose that you practice shooting while you walk. You hold the camera in one hand below the hip and shoot from that location, or from the neck in a strap, so you're shooting from the level of your stomach. The trick is really about choosing the moment when you shoot. Your body is moving forward at a steady pace as you walk, so you should rig for deep sharpness. The problem is that we also move slightly up and down, and like that wasn't enough also a bit from side to side as we advance on our feet. I will neglect the lateral movement as I regard that as being of minor importance. Then we have two directions to take in account: the forward motion and the up and down motion. The forward motion we have to keep – we are moving forward and there is no way to stop that, then we are no longer walking. The up and down motion may be minimized by shooting when the foot on the side you carry the camera is flat on the ground, on the down-step, so to speak.

Hitting the right moment when your foot is flat to the ground you are practically standing still with regard to the up and down movement, and it's time to hit the trigger. This will take some practice to really get working. You probably will have to tilt your camera, feel your foot on the ground and press the trigger. You may practice this at home too, walking in the yard and aiming for a window, or indoors if you happen to live in a house or a larger apartment. Try it out in crowds, nobody will notice and you are practicing your skills, really training to synchronize your own series of movements and actions, i.e., your walk and your hand movements.

Above there are three suggestions. You may come up with several others that may widen your repertoire of "tricks" to use. Remember that they are not recommended for everyday use. The idea is to play around with the camera, making you feel more secure handling it. Remember, it's just a game in order to better your handling of your equipment, but you might also capture some greats shots using these methods. A standard exercise is to snap a picture every day of the same view, or object. You either slowly change something in the frame, fiddle with the camera settings, use your cap to shadow parts of the frame, or something else. You essentially force yourself to start finding new aspects in a habitual snap. After one year you will be able to study a series of 365 images that essentially tells the story of how you got a bit better at making your pictures.

The problem with honing your skills, and aptitude, for keeping on with your photography is not really a problem. We must look at this as a chain of events leading up to a moment of emptiness inside each and every aspiring photographer. You don't get as many positive boosts as you used to by just keeping on with your usual manner of making photography.

You may be in the situation where you're playing too safe a game. If you come home every time you've been out with your camera with a handful of frames that you are satisfied with maybe, you are that good, but I stress that, maybe you're doing it wrong. If you're stuck in a rut for a couple of decades or more you must have realized that there are no easy victories to win. Then you have to become harder on yourself. You must drive yourself to the limits of your capabilities in a manner that will trigger your photographic content to flourish and evolve. You will not accept standing still at this point in your life. You have to develop in order to reach out for the possibilities that lies within your photography.

The thought that will linger in the back of your brain forever is: have I peaked as a photographer? Or, haven't you reached the spot where you could possibly be yet? You'll never know, as how long you're going to live. You may never be sure. If you've been a stable and reliable sports photographer, and you've never found out that your real calling was in macro imagesß of insects? Planning the battle of possible arenas where your skills will show themselves demands some kind of plan. There are countless possible pictures you could make, needless to say you cannot make them all. A good way to shorten the practice time is to look at your other interests, or hobbies. Are you interested in literature, chess, or something else? If you start with something you know a bit about it is easier to spot the possible scenes you want to shoot. Making a dramatic shot of a chess game will become much more menacing if you choose to snap your frame at a situation on the board that is a real twister, which the aficionados will understand. You will acquire more interest as you move along, maybe shooting the players talking to each other, closeups on a hand gripping a game piece, or just the shadows given by the game pieces over the board. You will discover that, as you move along, you will discover new angles, based on your original understanding of the scene you're trying to catch in your frames.

Maybe we will, at times, miss what our natural vocation is through the ways we act and live our lives, or, rather how we live and make photographs of our lives. It isn't easy to suggest what photographic ventures we have missed. Life pushes us in certain directions that seem so evident at the start, and for that matter not that much so towards the end. Why did I spend so much time making pictures of cracks in the walls of buildings? Why didn't I rather go for flowers, people, or sports like all the rest of the photographers? As a test of what is really is going on it is one sure way of getting to know if, and how, it works for you. It might even be an easy way of covering other stuff you got hung-up on when you get to be a bit more suspicious than you should have, if you get my drift.

The moment we are totally content with what we are doing is a whole other thing. We might regard the hunting for the perfect image as a kind of a quest for the holy grail. The pursuit of the perfect picture – never to be found, or made. Perhaps it is a whole range of things that are going to influence what we are thinking is the good way to chase the perfect image. It's like a farmer working to grow the perfect apples or potatoes. He may never find them, but during the work the farmer produces a whole lot of stuff. It is the same in photography, you might pass masterly images without even noticing them, and you are still occupied, chasing another motif, which makes you blind to the possible perfect image.

The chase for the perfect image is maybe the most significant feature in that action. When the chase gets so much more important than the end result. It's the way towards an end, where the end totally looses its importance. The road will be what develops the mind and your skills, and eventually even is the importance of your actions. We might even be severely mistaken. We might be so severely mistaken that in hindsight we might marvel at how mistaken we were regarding it. In a way we might take a chance at studying other photographer's style and, if observable, their manner of working. Remember that your road is your way to insight, but any road chosen demands a lot of work if you're going to reach anywhere near its end.

Aiming for something great is really all about setting a certain course of any activity. Without aiming somewhere it's hard to be sure of just in what direction you're heading. One thing you might be sure of is that you can't be sure of when you are heading in the "right" direction. If that's it, you will watch it reveal itself in due time, when the strategic aim is revealed. Then, and not before that, you will know what it was that you were after. If you persist on the route, it might be some emotional rewards waiting for you, at least. If there is more coming your way is really very hard to tell. You will know when you get there, at least then you will know.

Setting up goals for yourself, and achieving them, what about that? Yeah, that might work for some people, but I guess this way is not for everyone. I am more for a general direction: I'll go there! You'll encounter a lot of dragons and trolls, whether you'll meet a fair prince, princess or a chest of gold is not really sure at the start of any given project. There is so much that is uncertain and not within our own control in any direction, like in every other direction as well. We do not know, at the beginning of a journey what destinations will be reached and become fruitful. In that sense we will all be novices, since every new journey (photographic endeavor) we set out on is a new one. You might have learnt something earlier that is of importance here, but you don't know what and when.

The moment when you stop thinking about what you are doing you might have gotten some hang of it, or forgotten all about it. As you acquire new skills you will focus on these skills setting out to adopt even more new skills. When you look back there seems to be a seamless configuration of knowledge and skills within your current repertoire, but we know that you have acquired all that bit for bit. All that happened because you wanted to make a certain kind of images, and that was only the starting point.

How can you force yourself to maintain interest for years on end? I think photography in itself generates new interests as long as you keep at it. The key concept is about keeping with it, sure you will have dry spells when you don't make as many images. Don't worry, it is downtime okay, but that period is very important for your development. Think of it in the ways of that your brain is digesting all the new stuff you have tried to cram it with during the last couple of years. Making images is a kind of language and you might know it is when you suddenly have to say something in a language you haven't constructed a full sentence in since high school. Your tongue will feel awkward and your brain will seem blank, but after a while you are communicating! So, I think you should confidently move on, charge the batteries and get out of your house, scouting the streets for new motifs. You might even set out for the forests and/or the mountains on a quest to finally capture that image of a spellbinding rainbow. In general, when we grew an interest in something it's a lot like falling in love. At first, you're on fire, next it feels okay, and then we accept it as the natural state of things. Regarding "hobbies", we all know that they will come and disappear, some of them might remain. Your interest will shift from deep to shallow and your interests in general are doing things to you. Those interests have risen inside your mind and will linger there for some time. Still, at times, it might feel like photography calls your name. Almost like it's tempting you, a siren luring you in a way you cannot resist, and with a swooshing sound you're out the door! Isn't that strange? The drive comes from within and makes itself appear like something trying to direct us from a distance, calling for us?

A psychologist could probably explain how we go about presenting our inner calling as a matter we want to do. This must be some kind of construction remaining since we were cave men. I think that when you get possessed by that urge that you might be missing out on something if you don't make your usual walkabouts in your neighborhood at that instant, or some part of your life will go amiss.

There we might have it! We've made photography a part of our lives and when we don't make pictu-res for a couple of days, we feel that something is missing. Photography has become, if not our lives, but at least a major part, perhaps the very core, of our lives. We miss it when we don't practice it.

So; part of life, missing it! How did it advance that far? One day decades back in time, we fumbled with our first camera. Even reading parts of the manual, in order not to appear being dumb. Now look at us! Where did that fascination come from, and what is that image fixation doing in my mind? Am I just living in a bad B-movie like "The Return of the Body Snatchers"? The difference being that I want to 'snatch' the world in my images.

All the ideas you may create are things that you have processed beforehand in your brain before finally fixating them in your pictures. You're using all your senses, your skills, your experiences and your studies to produce a picture. That will be a synthesis of all the pictures you've ever seen, created, or just plain heard about. It's like all that backstory stuff suddenly merges into each new picture. Sometimes it gets better than all the previous ones, most of the time it gets different, and sometimes it gets worse than all of the other pictures in the world. It's like a kaleidoscope of broken parts from other people's images, your own, of course, and some you don't even remember that you have seen before, all mixed together into a maelstrom of fragmented pictures and it's all about you and your experience. This is how we all function, piecing together infinitesimal pieces of reality twisting it into a (possibly) new view of the idea of our reality. We will perhaps always call it "photography". If we try to cope with that tyrant, we may at best trot along with our hobby, with its ups and downs. If we try to fight it, quit it, or keep it nice and small, it won't work.

It's a lot like being a drug-addict, it's hard to kick the habit and you surely will lose some friends because of your behavior. It's not everybody who likes to be around someone who's constantly stopping in his tracks to snap some shots of decaying mortar on a wall and some straws of grass coming up through the tarmac. They might be thinking that's it like being out with a three year old in tow. You don't mind, since you just watched a guy across the street wearing a superman-suit, so you're trotting away to snap some shots of that guy and don't notice that your friend has sat down on a park bench, looking sad and forlorn.

You just run away from your friends. They even doubt if you're hearing what they are saying when you're walking side by side, since they listen to the almost constant rattling sounds from your camera shutter. You never look at your friend, but rather at the surroundings, scanning them constantly for new images to emerge. We know that new pictures emerge now and then, but please, constantly?

I reckon it's basically the same ideas we battle with all through life, so why should photography be different? The main issues are to decide if your objectives are realistic, or not. "To make the best photo ever" seems to land in the category of ambitions that are over the top. Even if you should succeed in making that singular special photo, it would probably not be regarded as the best photo ever, at least not until long after your death. So there's no sugar in that ambition! But, when we look at a more realistic objective it often seems to be dull and very simple, not that overwhelming achievements that we aspire to accomplish. Is it because we don't have a realistic view of your own capabilities, or what is it that turns the world upside down in that manner?

Maybe it's because we're not that good at analyzing our own capacity and skills, maybe even overestimating them a fair bit? Since we cannot judge ourselves from outside, we have to stick with the ideas and the thoughts that we never have done it like on a professional level before. Even if we really do not execute our photography like pros, but rather have to do with a "good enough" level that is too low to allow us into the group of the real pros. The bottom line is; do we really aspire to be amongst that crowd, or, do we want to set our bar a little lower?

No shame in that, it's even a bit more realistic and grown-up to realize what level we are able to aspire to be working at. Then we are able to, as a result of that reasoning, perhaps, be rather adult about it. You cannot always become the best when you start practicing something as a grown-up, you simply don't have the time. And really, following guys that tell us on the Internet how everything is going to be done? What's up with that?

In a manner of speaking we are going to become our worst enemies. We are so filled with ambition and most of us deny that; "Oh, no, I'm just dabbling at this, have nothing better to do, so I spend 400 hours a year making photographic images, plus an additional 300 hours processing them on my computer. What!? You spend that much time on something and you don't know what you're trying to get out of it? You must be kidding!"

It is always hard to decide when we are serious about what we really do. You realize that it is very rare for someone to come from nowhere and suddenly being the answer to all prayers within any chosen field of art. That creates a bundle of problems; we don't want to tell ourselves; "We are having fun, that's enough, oh no, there's talk about becoming a pro photographer in a year's time. We don't want to see all the boring "bread-and-butter-jobs" that will follow. Some think that they'll just be surfing around, making marvelous images and somehow, from heaven eventually, are going to get paid for doing that all day. That's really immature! I'm glad that I have always had a day-job writing and doing layout. Of course the thought of getting money doing something fun appeared to me as a young man when the thought of writing a bestselling book would erase all of my economic needs forever. We have all had our times being young and unrealistic!

If you ever catch me in the act of saying that I'll be the next great photographer, you're permitted to visit my humble abode and erase all my image files. I won't stop you, since I think you have the right to stop me from getting my head too swollen, it won't be any prettier at its double size.

Now, I'm a rather mature man, 70+, and I regard my salary days as being over. Sometimes I insist on doing some hours of "work", but since it's no necessity like in days past, I try to avoid it as much as possible.

I must confess, though, that I am sometimes of the impression that one of my images is great. That's about once a year, since some great photographer once stated that you (as a pro) might count one image that is extraordinarily good, and during a career of about 40, or 50, great images, that seem to be okay. I agree, the amazing images do not come in as big swarms as we want them to appear. Sometimes they sneak upon us, and afterwards we don't really know from where they came. So, now they are here, and it's only to accept them, like all good things in life. Don't brace yourself against them, if you feel the urge to press the trigger, do so. Don't hesitate, or put it off until later, because the then and there don't do any repetitions of that moment in time. Grab that image by its tail, and maybe get sorry later when you look at the result, rather than not act and be a guy telling stories of a lost image, in the same vein as fishermen talking about big fish that they almost succeeded in landing.

Never even think about rejecting the moment when it comes knocking at your door (or, in your mind). You will regret it! You don't want to willingly make your life harder as a photographer than it already is. Take the chance, click the trigger! You'll never be sorry if you do, but you're sure to be sorry if you don't. The images you acquired are possibly the best you had the chance to make at the moment. So don't fret over their quality, they could have been worse, they could have been better, but they are not, so instead be happy that you got a couple of frames, rather than none. Keep in mind; one dollar is always more than none. It goes for images too, when you're looking into the future; what do you really see? Do you see yourself like some kind of guru of photography? Do you picture yourself having some traces of that guru-ship today? Do your photo friends listen to your ideas on photography, or don't they? If your friends do listen, you might have picked up on some fruitful ideas, concepts or mannerisms that serve you well. You have educated yourself within the visual arts in a way. Then you are to be congratulated, you might even have a solid foundation to build your own photography on! You might understand images in a manner much more sophisticated than your peers. You might even have acquired your knowledge some time ago so it has had time to mature and reflected on, not just some copying of books or courses.

When you make a lot of photos, publish some of them in social media and are getting some "likes" it boosts your ego, more than anything. You don't really know why people "like" your images in photo groups. In some way you might get a kick out of those "likes". You must remember, though, that it's not the art world that run the Facebook groups, it's ordinary people creating a "water hole, or, camp fire" for other ordinary people. If you get a lot of "likes" it does not necessarily mean that you're making awesome images – it only means that you are mainstream in that particular group, perhaps in combination with your friends giving you supportive "likes".

The thing with presenting your images to anyone, excluded your mom, or, yor partner, because they'll probably support you at any given time, is more complicated than you would imagine. But, what about all the others? Some comments from when I have shown some images to friends give a hint about what is spinning around within the heads of others. The first, and most common one, is about presentation: "Should there be a thick black frame around the image like that?". The second, very common, comments: "Is that in Barcelona? No, it couldn't be." A third one is about the choice between black and white and color presentation: "Why do you choose to present it in black and white, color is so much more relevant! Black and white seems so old fashioned". It is understandable that comments like that do not allow for me getting so much wiser. That may concern that many of my friends in social media do probably not have any strategies when commenting images. They probably have no idea what to say, anyhow. They were probably commenting to get rid of me.

Image critique

What I like to concentrate on here is that random people in your vicinity don't necessarily deliver good image critique. Members of your local photo club do not, as a rule, do that either. So, who are you going to find to criticize your images? Obviously, you have to get hold of someone who knows the ins and outs of photography; and don't have to bill you for the advice. You might get billed if you have that kind of budget. Think about it. Do you want to pay a person you never heard of with no visible CV, no website, etc.? I don't think a person, in a way a random guy, with a lot of ambition and self-esteem is so much better at criticize your images than your ordinary photo-chums.

The problem, and challenge, is to get in contact with the right people. There are not many of them out there, so they'll be hard to find. There are too many "know-it-alls" but, not that many of them are to be trusted giving good advice, good tips or, whatever you ask of them. As always, good help is hard to find! When you sometimes come by one, they have to move to another part of the country and cannot continue to be your constantly accessible discussion partner anymore. I guess that's how life is and you just have to start anew. You cannot stop doing what you are doing just because of what other people choose to do in their lives. You must go on with your quest for that perfect image, wherever it will appear! At least in that casual manner that is more relevant than usual most of the time.

In that quest you may allow disturbances that you cannot influence, people that block you or those who think that your work is below par. Who are they to be given permission to judge, as they, it appears, just go on about what they like, or dislike? The hard case with photography is that there is no standard, like the standard meter in silver in Paris, France, used as basis of measurement. It could be said to be the mother of all meters in the world. They are supposedly as long as the meter in France. If we could get a standard photo like that to compare with! Yeah, I know, the diversity of photography requires a gigantic number of standard images stored in Paris, France, to give ample comparisons. We are out there with anyone who dares to say anything about photographic images at all. They become some kind of "experts" if you listen to them, or take their given advice.

So, how do you think the photographic industry is feeling at the moment? Too many self-ordained "experts" are feeding on doing courses, and/or, seminars at the moment, telling everybody else what they might do.

The reality is that this is bad for all photographers. I'm fascinated by the "cocksure" attitudes displayed in some groups in social media by someone who bought a camera some years ago and now is an "expert" on every shape or form of the photographic display. Nobody's that fast a developer in a new field of work. The images they display themselves are at best replicas of some well-known artist's work. That is a sad development indeed! I reckon that that kind of people have always been there, giving out advice, even billing you for it. You must even argue that the writer of this text is one amongst them, giving unsolicited advice on what advice not to listen to! The difference today compared to earlier is that there are so many hobbyist photographers wanting to grow better and they are even willing to pay for developing their skills. Then they deserve teachers or, scouts, who know what they are teaching. It is all too easy to develop a concept and start selling it today.

I've tried the "praise" concept in other domains of life. Find a way to say something nice about everybody's contributions, do that consistently for some length of time. Even if you are exaggerating, people like being praised, being looked upon as doing good work. When you're praised the purpose of the praise will raise you to another level, you will become more willing to take risks and not always play it safe. The person that is praised will feel good following that praise.

The way that method worked many years ago within a project group where everybody was praised, all of the time. Someone finally commented: "You're praising us, whatever we do, don't you?" The combined work results were a whole lot better than when we only expected everyone to deliver without praise. The group became fully functional and worked swiftly and precisely. That was indeed a big shift compared to the situation before the "praises-campaign" started. Just saying, it doesn't need much to change a sad story into a successful one. I venture that if I started coaching some 20 hobby photographers, after a year they would have become much better photographers, if I just praise them.

What about the "false prophets"? It might be only me, but I think they multiply each month. It's not that I don't like that people are so sure that they set out to give advice and teach others. They have the right to do that, but I feel sorry for the ones, who are so insecure that they want to know the "tricks" of the trade from people who started making images later than themselves. Okay, they might be slow learners.

Okay, let's not dwell on the "false" prophets any longer. They are a kind of effect in any growing sector of human endeavor. People want in on some money on all ends of the production of your photography!

When all the irritating stuff is dealt with, and gone, then we can start with the stuff that is important. So, there's a lot of decisions to be made in order to get along the happy and productive trail of photography. Not until then, when all the irritating loose ends are dealt with. That means we all have stuff to work with before starting the REAL image-making. Then we will be alone to start anew in our own photographic endeavors. You listen to that; do you hear what it sounds like? It's like we are victims of circumstances and not citizens of free will and enterprise! All the stuff that is blocking us is only a photographer's block, and nothing else.

We are letting our thinking to block us way before we start shooting. That is not what we ought to do, we should just start the camera and go on shooting until the memory card is full! No excuses are valid. If you think too much about how to shoot, you won't make pictures, you may very well be teaming up with photographic theory, and theory alone.

Let's be honest, it's not time for that yet. The theory must be based on something. Yes, it seems to be based on photographs others have made. Wouldn't it be better if it was based on the images you or I have made? Closer to home, don't you think?

I think we make up a lot of arguments that aim at explaining why we cannot go out making pictures this day, or tomorrow. The most important thing ever is to leave the house and meet the world, checking up on what is going on, finding pictures in it before they disappear. Yes, I do overstate it a bit, or else we would not catch the drift. We are exaggerating things that result in blocking us from going out there and making pictures. If we don't try to renew ourselves, we probably would be making the same image over, and over again. That would be the end of that story. We would be done for the day and could start looking forward unto tomorrow. With little doubt, only the futile hopes of that we will make a set of marvelous images the next day, and the day after that. No one is going to slap us then. That is a rather hard manner to live the life of a hobby photographer. Why this has to be so complicated is a riddle to me. We want to make pictures, we want to go out there, and sometimes we don't do as we wished, or had planned. Okay, there might be something coming up that you just have to attend once in a while, you have to take care of your job and your family. But, what about all the other times? I see that I may lose interest in going out if I think I'm going to make a lot of pictures, so I have adjusted my habits a bit. That means that I carry a camera in my hand most of the time that I'm away from home. Even if I just leave home in order to pick something up at the grocers.

That has helped me a lot. I'm out there minding my business (never really go out just to shoot pictures), camera in hand, and oops, I made some frames! So, it's mainly about taking charge of your own situation! No one will do it for you, so there's only one person to do it! I reckon that it becomes easier over time to hold on to your promises to yourself. You don't have to be super disciplined to manage to create a steady stream of images, just more conscious about that you are managing your own weaknesses. We know everything about them and we are aware that they might bring us down in our work with our photography. Whatever direction that takes us it will be a new one since every step we take along the path of wandering indicates that it's never too late to pick up on the good things we encounter in life. We absolutely have to develop a skill when we go about getting older, we could not just be happy about what we already knew or could do so far in our lives. There is always room for more knowledge!

We are trying get hold of something that we think

is important in life so that we have to sacrifice something else to get there, or, do we really? What if there is other stuff we can sacrifice in this manner? Or rather be doing something completely different? What do we want to do so bad that it can't exist simultaneously with our photography hobby? Is it just excuses not to keep up with our highly set objectives? Are we unrealistic about our goals?

Maybe our appetite for objectives is by far greater than our capabilities to see them through in real life? It seems relatively modest when we set forth to make one (1) image a day the coming year. In reality, we might break that sequence the second week we're at it. Are we so incomparable with our own way of setting goals in a realistic manner for our activities? There seems at least to be some discrepancies in that neighborhood, don't you agree?

I really don't know why we are trying to sabotage our own activities in this manner, but I spy evil forces at play. Maybe not in the way that I would argue that there really are evil forces at play, but since it is a bit away from making it harsh and voluntary. We don't have to do it since we earn our living from another career. We don't have to do photography for our living, so it might create passages in our lives when we are not doing ANY photography since somebody is paying us to do other stuff. It might be good for us or it may ruin the skills we want to pick up. Really? Remember how ten years may pass without you riding a bicycle and you sit up on one and your (complex) skills have not been lost at all! I think it's the same with photography, you acquire a certain set of skills, they might become rusty over time, but you really never lose them. They're just hiding to come back to you when you call them back. Really, skills like this are all in your body. Your camera is a prolongation of your eyes, and to back them up is your brain. They are all there, and they are ready to start making photographs.

If you're following me so far, you'll have a breeze taking in what I'm going to explain now. Why is it that we make it hard for ourselves to go out and shoot freely with our cameras? Does it have to do with the fact that it is a hobby and we don't want to become "nerds", or obsessed with a mere hobby? Whatever the reason(s) we have to do something about it. It's not about feeling uneasy carrying around a "ready-to-shoot" camera any more. We're far beyond that, for sure, but there are some inhibitions left and you've got to free yourself from them, or you'll be forever crippled as a photographer. You will maybe avoid your camera, start fuzzing around with stuff that don't produce any pictures.

That's not the way it was meant to be. You should be eager to get out there in the world and shoot until your memory card gets full and you've got to go home and back it up. Why is it that photography is something we are interested in and even though we might leave that interest be for several weeks and months? Are we scared of a sudden success, when people around us start to criticize our work? Wasn't that what we wanted in the first place? Maybe not? We may have wished for a role as a good photographer that everybody automatically respects and don't patronize. That might be kind of a blissful place to be, but why don't we stop being so paranoid about our eventual success and just keep on doing images? I think of Vivian Meier, who kept on making images for decades during the analogue era. She didn't develop most of her rolls of film. She wasn't able to give herself feedback on what work she had accomplished. But she kept on going, knowing, perhaps, one of the principal rules; the importance of steadily making pictures.

In this part some things like why we seem to oursel-ves have been discussed. Some of the main features discussed above are:

- Shoot everyday
- Shoot everywhere

Do you make new images?

The question whether you make new images or, are just repeaingt a "winning" concept time and time again is an important question to put sometimes. I have come by critique of photographers on some exhibitions that says: "she makes the same image over and over again". It's a comment that points to repetition like it has to be a bad thing. The repetition is a way of working, to squeeze all the possibilities you may find out of a subject. To really "milk" it for all the probable gains and perspectives it might contain. It is an ordinary manner of working with ideas, really. To go for different possibilities, all the way down to the bare bones of the matter. I can't find another, more honest, way to focus on that subject matter. When you make a statement like that repetition is bad, you must be kidding!

Repetition may be argued to be the mother of excellence, and whatever we do is an on-going education. We repeat, trying out new angles, make new attempts at something we tried earlier. That is the way to learn and "practice makes perfect"! You shouldn't even have to use a viewfinder. You ought to know where the picture is in front of you by heart, like a ninja. So, you watch, you aim, make the picture and it's a done deal! At least until you get home and start checking the results on your computer screen. Then what you think you got unravels itself into being something completely different. Not bad enough to erase, but saving and keeping in mind until the next time you get out there. Tomorrow, perhaps?

What about this constant urge to get out and make more pictures? If you don't like pictures, you're not a photographer, it's as easy as that. You make pictures in order to be able to call yourself a photographer. Although some think you have to make "good" images to earn that epithet, some don't even care. They call themselves photographers the moment they leave the store with a camera in a parcel, or in a strap around their neck. I argue that you must at least make a few pics, don't you?

So, in order to be able to call yourself a photographer you make pictures. You don't, like I do in these texts, just keep on talking about photographers and images. On the other hand, if you've made your "masterpiece", you cannot hope for anything more, so what should you do then? Should you start painting, sculpting, write a series of essays on photography, or continue making images? Since the chance that you will be able to recreate your "masterpiece" and be able to make another as great a picture is slim you might have arrived at a dead end situation, even if the possibilities still are out there. Even if, like it's said, lightning doesn't strike twice in the same spot, it might happen. Even if it's only about proving the vagueness of the improbability in a way. So, if you keep on keeping on, you might get there a second time and catch the great picture number two in your lifetime. That's the way you have to do it!

Maybe photography is not all about making awesome images. It might be about the more philosophical aspects of creating images of the world around us. To really occupy yourself trying to solve "the riddle" in what you see might be an occupation that could drive you further. By driving I mean moving yourself far out from your mind, leaving the small world that used to be your own and reaching out, through a photographic image, to a much larger world for everybody to discover within your imagery.

Every time someone tells you that you shouldn't, that's just the time for you to do it. Those belittling "you shouldn't" or "you ought to" are the critics manner of trying to tell you that you don't understand, you're not capable, and that is why you shouldn't listen to them speaking. Who's going to prove them wrong? Of course you are that person! Everybody who other people don't regard capable should rise as one person and prove the critics wrong.

I assume that since some people are insecure of their own capabilities, they want to push that over on to others. "If I can't or daren't, nobody else should either!". So, they really are belittling others because of their own feelings of shortcomings instead of taking on the battle with their own shortcomings. Their negativity becomes a weapon to attack everything that threatens their own position. But, it's really about what they are perceiving as their position, defining a right to criticize others' work at their own will instead of using that willingness to forward constructive critique. That would really be a more fruitful manner to handle it, for everybody concerned, not at least the recipients of that ungrounded critique. For them it will work as a support and not as a way of undermining everything they aim at doing with their manner of regarding photography. So, my advice is not to listen to people who take for granted that they are doomed to be all over the place, given free, but unwanted, advice. If you do like photography and have ideas of your own, you're generally speaking wasting time with that kind of people. Just ignore them!

One way of managing reckless criticism like that is to more or less ignore it. Some people want to say a lot of stuff, commenting on things around them, but not because they really have any expertise in the matter, rather that they would like to "help". Ignorant critique is sadly no help at all, and if you listen to stuff like that you will only get confused. In order to be a bit more annoying, if possible; to be confused is better than being nothing at all. In short, don't mind people nagging at you, don't make it personal, don't let them bring you down with their unreflected comments. They know no better, or they wouldn't have spoken at all, but held their peace, and shut up. You see, they're getting at you until you tell yourself that you don't care what they say. Obviously, you do, and you reckon that you'll come back at them. But, why bother? You don't want to become a victim of circumstances you cannot control, do you?

Now, over to something slightly more interesting! Why do we just "know" how to create awesome images? In a way, we have some kind of "taste" regarding photography, we may often recognize what is in the images. That's things we learn growing up. Why is it that not everybody has that grasp of drawing, painting, creating music, or, practice photography from the similar educative journey in school? Wouldn't it be very much nicer if everybody could keep their fingers out of other people's business? Sometimes we tend to look at images of others and be too harsh on them, just because we regard them as being rude, or occupying too much room within the public space. That might be a self-indulged privilege. Privileges like that are seldom handed out, so someone has zoomed in on himself and has converted himself into a self-proclaimed judge of all others in a similar field of art. If we don't are careful these guys will be gaining ground everywhere, and we don't like that to happen, do we? My advice is to just ignore them, don't bother to accept their occupancy of all that space. It's suffocating!

That isn't the worst things they might accomplish. They have a possibility to gain followers. Then you're really in for it! So, if you're looking for a lot of work you really don't need, you ought to express some critique and then in no way back it up. But you cannot run from your foundation. Since you'll have to back it up, eventually. When all the questions start popping up and you really hadn't thought it through, had you? It was in a way someone else who had designed for you, or your thoughts, you only uttered something smart, but didn't and then there was tumult and a lot of angry phone calls. And so on!

The manner in which you present critique is, of course, important. If you don't explain what you're aiming at with your critique it tends often to appear as an attack on the person who created the material. I always explained to my staff that I did not criticize THEM as persons, but rather that I was disappointed with the quality of their work, since I expected more from them, knowing how good they were.

The way we present our pictures is the way we present ourselves. If you do inferior prints and try to present them on an exhibition, you're going to find that out the fastest way. Nobody likes things that are a little bit off. But it might have been 'the concept', and you have to make room for that. That 'off-ness' sparkles an awareness of dissonance, a component that should not be there. Just that little bit off the right track, so it's almost perfect, but not really on the spot. That is somewhere in the vicinity of Barthes' 'punctum'. That enables doubts to enter the equation of your trying to hit the targets i.e. the mind of the viewer. That is a situation that is tough to master, so make your outmost in your presented images; were they really supposed to look like this, or is that just a coincidence that they came out looking like this? If you don't know you must confess that you have no idea about what you are doing. Maybe it's time you went through your routines again? Somehow chance may help you, but always make an inward note to yourself that chance might be your friend, but really, is chance your friend all the time? The future viewers do not need to know, but you, as the author, have to be sure about how your images were created.

The aid of chance is no new-comber to creating images, or, even art in general, so there's no shame in letting chance having its finger within the game. The manner of handling chance as a dear friend is the way to go about this process. You should always remember that chance is no enemy, but rather a somewhat hard to handle acquaintance that you should work on getting to know a whole lot better. Welcome chance whenever you meet it, don't get irritated, you have the possibility of erasing whatever result chance brings you, but my advice is to wait a bit. When looking at your frames after 3-4 months later you might be in the mood to appreciate them more than just an hour after making them. So, go ahead and erase if you think chance did not help at all.

I wonder why we even should bother about remarks from other people if they are not "experts" on photography. Not even if they are, is it really certain that they know the important stuff that may help you and me further along in our work with image creating? Things that may help us a whole lot when we are trying to theorize around what we do with our images. My own theorizing starts at the moment when I raise my camera out of my shoulder bag, catching the lift down to the ground floor and then, en route, making images all the way down to the subway station. There is nothing more to it. You don't need to have spicy ideas about what you are doing. What you've got to do is with you all the time, everywhere and without stop. Photography is the way you breathe, the manner in which your heart beats, and the way your eyes shine when you're hunting for what you would argue is going to become a good picture.

If you can stand tall and proud since the pictures you've made all are great, that is really nice, if you can't, you have to revise your way of using your camera. In what way you might not know at the moment. You can adjust how you work at a later date. You don't have to, but you want to, don't you?

The way we try to go about making our pictures is of course an individual path. Most people go about it in different ways, without giving it a thought. There must be some common factors in this activity. After all, we're talking about creating pictures! Not all is good if you tap into your main source of creativity and start wondering, one way or another, if this really is a part of who you are. Where ever your inspiration comes from, never forget that it's you making these pictures! Don't you ever forget that!

One thing you should not show anyone is if you set up pictures in the style of someone else, bit for bit. Copying, if you will. That is plagiarism and however unblemished your conscience is it is frowned upon. If you show a picture in public that is too "inspired" by someone else you might even be prosecuted for infringement of copyright laws. So, don't even show pictures like that, not even to a "friend". If you use these pictures as a manner of understanding the technique it's a whole other ballpark. You are using the making of images in the style of someone else for educational purposes. You might be "influenced" by someone, meaning that it is possible to say that you must have studied that person's images in order to make your own.

Then we could discuss if sunsets are some kind of plagiarism, since I don't notice any differences between the ones I spot on Internet. Maybe natural phenomena like sunsets are archetypical symbols, and as such may never be really be subject to copyright in the usual sense. Maybe, unless if it was the case, there would appear a series of court cases going on everywhere. If you're so in sync with the rest of the photographic community that your images look like all the rest, or, like a "copy" of someone else's image, don't publish it! Even if you tell the story about how you were practicing to make this kind of motifs, that might be misunderstood as you being a "fraud" artist-wise. Keep those images in a folder that states that it was part of an educational purpose only. Then you will remember when you're feeling tempted to publish them. You will, of course, have acquired knowledge following that direction.

What kind of images are the most influential? Of course we have the pictures from the news media, like the running naked girl 'The Napalm Girl', Kim Phúc, photographed on June 8, 1972, by AP photographer Nick Ut, 'The Liberation Kiss' shot in Paris by Robert Doisneau and Robert Capa's shots from the Spanish Civil War. These images are documentary and at the same time reports from events that concern a lot of people, in this case different aspects of war and migration as a result of war. These pictures tell us about some stories under development, but also about the necessity of being where things happen. Somebody has caught the strongly dramatic content — being there is the most important way to be able to transmit that. The photographers hanged around the people for a month or two, and sometimes considerably longer, waiting for that moment — and that special image. Others are images that the photographer has happened to detect, while not being on a special mission. All of the images mentioned above have been considerably influential, since they tell us stories about people and of people's lives. Since we ourselves are human beings we tend to understand these images and can understand the stories contained within them.

As far as photographic images go, they may surface everywhere you happen to go. Always do your best, within the moment, to "art" your image up, thinking about framing, focus — non focus, diagonals, black and white possibilities and so on. The image you make during your customary photo-sessions on any day, or most of your days, might be the image of your life. Maybe you have not succeeding in making it yet, but next time you release the shutter it might be your big moment, at last!

There is always hope, or else you would become heartbroken with the tens of thousands of images you have made that did not come out awesome. The hope is still there anyway, isn't it? Sure is. You have to make your masterpiece today, or tomorrow, no one can tell. Maybe the reality is that you probably will grind on with your photography for years to come and sometimes one of your photo-friends will make a positive remark on some of your images. You are going to live on that praise for a long time! It does not matter, because making that image was just the run of the mill, but it is nice when someone recognizes your effort, and says something nice about it afterwards. It is about the feeling of possibilities your stand in front of every time you raise your camera and aim it.

So, it is not really about becoming rich, or famous. It's really just about shooting, if you are going to stick with this habit of yours. I know it might seem awkward imagining the thought that you would someday find yourself amongst the ones making awesome images, but I reckon the ones that get that recognition might have thought like that a long time ago. Maybe they have not appeared and they went on into the world and simply amazed it? Maybe the result was so obvious from the start? Since talent is like a godsend it is not evenly distributed within the population, or even the photographic population. You might get good, but the question is whether you have what it takes to become a photographer with an almost constants flow of awesome images, without talent that is not doable, at least not according to my thinking.

Why worry about fame and fortune that might never come, isn't it enough to just make a lot of photographs and have fun doing it? Maybe we all want to have that open road (we think) into glory as an inspiration? Maybe it's about having goals set by others. If you're not famous, you're nobody. We know we are somebody, all of us. I reckon that if we did photography trying to live by it, maybe we would be more rational about it. Nobody will pay me to make a photo, I have to work in another line of work. Since we don't have to get any income to survive the last outpost lingering in the distant future is maybe fame and fortune (hopefully). If we work hard as photographers, we would be artified every day, just like in the ordinary working life. Are you worth what we pay you? We make the mistake regarding photography that we are worth our pay, but that pay is coming from a steady job, not from selling photographic images one at a time. That is a big mistake to do, and we are a doing a lot of falling into that pit of mistakes.

It is hard to tell if we are victims of our own vanity or, if we are victims of other people's view on vanity. Basically vanity is always the same kind of vanity. We might be less aware of it, but it's basically the same emotions that we have to cope with. Even if we know that the game is over on our part, we still want to pretend that all the possibilities are there for us, they're all still entirely intact. The longing for recognition is one thing we are constructed to encompass, in a way during our upbringing forced to adhere to, like it's important for all, when it's basically important to a chosen few.

If you can rid yourself of the plague of a quest for success, whatever that even is, you should do fine. Do your thing and don't listen to attentively to what others say about you, or about your photography. Then you'll be okay and able to have fun with your photography, playing around with it like it was supposed to be. Photography wasn't invented to become a hassle. The Daguerreotype was intended by the French Government to be bought from Niépce's son and Daguerre presented the invention to the world (with the exception of Great Britain, where an agent for Daguerre patented it) as a free gift. This was designed as a guarantee that the method was going to be accessible throughout the world. That could be said to have been very insightful. Imagine how it had been if the secrets of photographic technology had landed behind locks with limited access to them! The way we treat photography now, at least most of us, is mainly the "black box" style. We don't even care what is under the shell of the body of the camera. At least as long as it gives us what we want. If that is 16 MP-frames or 36 MP-frames or other possibilities that might influence our photography doesn't matter. Some of us might be more interested in the contents of the camera body, but not everyone cares. We read about what the camera body can do, but most of us doesn't use half of the gadgets and possibilities.

In this part some things like keep on keeping on have been discussed. One of the main features discussed above are:

• Don't get rid of your inner three year old kid, always wanting to look atthings.

Technology Is Never the Message

Marshal McLuhan, who coined the phrase: "the media is the message" didn't mean, I think, that the singular technological features were what contained the message, but rather that the media, like photography today, for example, has its limitations and that the transit into digital technology didn't have to do with what kind of service a certain make of camera equipment could offer. Photography is the media, transmitted along a variety of communication corridors like: blogs, books, websites, bulk e-mail and exhibitions. They all present the images in a slightly different context. That context may color the images so they really transform, depending on the media you are meeting them in /on. They are still the original images, we accept that, but, at the same time, they appear to be slightly different. I think that it is like when you meet someone in a place you hadn't expected or, if they are wearing a strange set of clothing you have never seen them in before.

Basically, it appears that the very same images you are encountering in slightly different media channels have changed a bit. Every media channel has its own 'persona' that color the images they transmit. In some respect they appear to still being the very same images, but appearing different as they have been smitten by the characteristics of the 'channels' they appear in. So, if the very same subject is treated by different photographers, the author might be regarded as a different media channel for the motif. We don't often think it odd if the image comes out a little different. We regard that as natural. So, maybe the channels work in the same manner, 'branding' the images in the same way? Each and every photographer may be regarded as a 'channel' that sets his 'mark' or 'brand' on his images, very similar to the way a 'media channel' works. According to Marshal McLuhan the media channels work through 'coloring' the 'message'. So, my images from a forest are never the same as yours from that same forest, made the very same day. They might be related to one another, but not really the identical image that we watched a while back. Along the road transmitting these images all the way to some viewers at an exhibition, on Facebook, a blog, a website, or sending that image via e-mail. All this 'travelling' for the image will influence the image in a manner very similar to people when they are conveying a message and using their way of expressing themselves.

It is not easy to get around the fact that what you're saying is what makes the difference. The channels (we) furnish the messages (the images) that are then presented within one of the channels. I reckon the channels (media) has its own manner of getting under our skins. We think we are able to look through everything that is wrapped into the message as it reaches us. But can we? Probably the location when we encounter images have like McLuhan argued, colored the images so they appear a bit different, (without really being that), depending on the channels they appear in. They are raising different emotions within the viewer depending on the different circumstances.

Do we ever think about the impact of the "wrapping paper"? Like when you were young and your parents asked you not to hang out with certain friends, since they the parents thought those friends were "bad" for you? If you would want to become a "rock'n roll star" photography is probably both the best and at the same time being the worst option for it. It's the best since you literally don't have to acquire any language in order to get the images you want. On the other and, the images also reveal where you have been in the sense that you have never been in "forbidden" places, or at least in the wrong places at the right moment. Legally you might get hunted, but there's just a few areas where that will happen.

Your camera is a magnified fortification of your eyes, so train yourself to really see, really examine life in a constant manner. If you go about it in a steady progression, then possibly, you will note some development over time. It should come automatically and trigger you grabbing your camera.

The way we include the entire world in our images is a matter of how we can deal with the positive things in some were rotten situations in life, and within our photography. This is one way of getting the images done and another is getting it done right.

Why all this discussion of pros and cons? Is it really

important and / or does it really matter? Do we ever really make an effort to make the "best images" that we are capable of? It's up to your own conscience to decide if you're constantly up there in the 90 percent plus of your ability, or if you share images that maybe are lurking around at the 75 percent line of your capabilities to execute 'good' images? You know that there is nothing forcing you to show those sub-par images. And anyway you continue doing it? Is it possible that social media like Instagram, LinkedIn and Facebook, and the likes, have something to do with your choice? Where would you go to exhibit your images if you didn't hang out on social media? Maybe in your own photo club? That would not hold for like 60 images per month, would it? If you are ten guys meeting once a month and everyone brings 60 images, that will be A LOT of images to look at, maybe even coming up with something to say about some of them. I gather that if you would present your images in "real life" it would be a whole lot fewer than that, wouldn't it? That's different compared to the wide furrows you are entitled to on Facebook and the like. Why do I point this out? Is it because it's bad, or possibly harmful for your development as a photographer?

On the one side it is bad since mass production almost always means a cut in the level of perfection, i.e., lack of quality, at its worst. On the other hand it might be a good thing to mass production since you learn to get stuff out of your hands and don't fiddle around with them forever. Which is the most important of these? I reckon that if you do both, in moderation, it might bestow some good on your photographic skills in the short run. I think you need to have long periods of reflection over the quality of your work, during periods when your output isn't that high. Then you'll have time to think, experiment, not producing at that intensive rate.

So, maybe working at a slower pace, more concentrated studies of your results and matching it to what you think you want to achieve. And try to be critical about your own images. There are a couple of possibilities:

A; you think your images are awesome,
B; you have already made a similar image,
C; they look like some images you have seen by another painter or photographer,
D; the images you are looking at is a combination of the two options above – looking both like some other person's images and at the same time, looking like some images you have made earlier,
E; it's a really good image, and you should be proud of yourself! The chance that you image will end up in this category is slim, you must remember that. Most of the images we make are, in a way, some kind of remakes of already existing concepts, visualized by you, or by others. Don't worry, as long as you realize this, it is a natural part of your training. The dangerous part is when you don't see it and get too cocky about images that really are nothing to brag about.

It is hard to be cocky and brag about your images in a good way. So, you have better not being over confident about your hobby. You don't have to live in poverty and squalor until your images are "discovered". Frankly, what is the probability for that happening today, when everybody is a "photographer"? It might seem confusing that the images that you think are great don't get much recognition. Maybe it's about that you haven't reached out there yet. Remember the possibilities to make books and exhibitions? Or, if you're that inclined, try to hold classes. A good measure of your status as a photographer is whether people sign up for your classes, or not. Everybody you know already think they're much better than you, so they won't sign up for your classes. The rest of the world has never heard of you.

The way to come around problems like that is to gain recognition, by making books, doing exhibitions and writing articles in trade journals is a way into the business-side of every trade. I reckon it is the same in the photographic trade. You have to ask yourself if it is important for you to gain recognition, so important that you're willing to spend valuable time away from your photographing trying to become some kind of photo guru. If you have had really profound insights into the do's and don'ts of photography it would be known by now, don't you reckon? Haven't you been talking to anyone about photography in the last decade? I am not trying to be nasty, but have you done anything to support your skills, and spreading the knowledge of your skills? Are you good at explaining stuff to other people? Do you have educational skills? Have you ever been a sports coach, a teacher (even a sub), an information officer, or writing journalist? The latter are trades that will help you, if you want to switch in on teaching others what you already know about photography. If you have nothing in your background that correlates with what I wrote earlier in your background, don't you fret, you might be a natural. You can ride a bike, right? Have you taught your kids how to ride one? How did you go about it, and how did that work out for you? Did the kids manage to ride their bikes? Were you instrumental in teaching them? Why not? Didn't they listen to you because you got irritated? That's not a good sign, you know. Why do you think you would get your teaching to work better with adults, they won't take abuse like that? They'll get downright angry right back at you, maybe even leave your class, demanding their money back.

So, I think that if you haven't had a lifelong desire to develop skills in teaching you ought to abandon that right now. Start writing a couple of texts with some photographic trade journal in mind and take it from there. You might make an impact on people without being a face-to-face teacher. You should save a lot of time for your own photographic endeavors. Maybe the ways we work with photography will fill us with some of the feelings that will bring us some of the emotions we are so good at embracing, but the more we have learnt we fathom that it isn't exactly the same as if we get better at teaching others some of the skills we possess. Every sports star does not become a great coach, they know how to play themselves, but there is a certain set of skills required to teach others to do that, really demanding a separate set of skills that not everybody possesses.

The skills needed to teach what you know to someone else doesn't come automatically at a certain level of accomplished skills. No, we will be looking for other challenge, won't we? We are out there trying to catch "the theater of the world" on a memory card. Why don't we just keep at it, trying our best to become the best we possibly can at that? There are still some sets of 5.000 exposures to deal with in the near future, before we kick the bucket. Before that we will no doubt happen to get into new discussions on photography, dream about new exposures and new ideas in a continuous stream of images and thoughts about them. Like we never have sorted any images out, we will sort our external hard drives out, trying to look at all the images we ever backed up. If we look at these images upside down or flipped them sideways, do they look different? I have flipped some images sideways since some of them seem to make more sense in their composition that way. Of course you should only do that with images that do not contain any text elements since in that case you will be caught red-handed. The text elements will reveal that you have flipped the image – sometimes the image is really improved – sometimes it is not.

The main thing is still to aim at the photographic images you haven't made yet, the ones to amaze us! No one can stay on the summit with images that are 15-20 years old. Maybe if you're 90 now, but hardly if you are younger than that. It's a struggle, but you're only as good as the last set of images you made. Photography is in that sense a commodity that may, or may not, age badly.

Problems you might experience at times, while trying to develop your skills, honing your skills, if you wish, are that what you might regard as improvement does not necessarily be based on the same criteria as others consider important when judging photographic images. This may be ground for misunderstandings, but not to worry; you don't have to care much about that. You are in this game in order to ameliorate your own skills, regardless of what others think you ought to improve. Regardless that your objectives and the objectives of other people might coincide, you might have the possibilities to take advantage of some of the aspirations of your photographer friends. They might be interested in the same things as you – or they might already have mastered what you are interested in getting to grips with. If so, don't hesitate to ask their advice about how they went about acquiring their skills, or knowledge. Did they attend classes, read about photography and practicing, or did they just go all in experimenting, until they got to grips with the things they wished to know? To state the obvious, no man is an island, and having people around you that are interested in developing the same skills and techniques as you are a good thing you have going. You have to see to it that you know what the friendly photographers around you are doing. They might be able to help you – but, remember, they don't have to!

The way to increase your abilities to make photography is just only the void. There are lots of ways you might acquire knowledge, and shortly you have investigated how, when and whom. Now you're ready to take advantage of your fellow photographers. Don't go about that in a bad, and greedy manner, help them if they ask for help, and you are suddenly in a position to give help to others.

No one likes a person who just keep asking for favors, and never gives anything back. That's why you have to be open about what you're trying to accomplish and how others may help you (if they want to). This is really about normal, decent behavior, nothing more, and nothing else. If you only want help and never is really supportive people around you will stop giving you help. You can't really blame them, since they only have to give and never get anything in return. The relationship must be on equal terms. Be generous with your ideas and normally people around will be generous right back at you! Then, you and your fellow photographers will benefit mutually, from helping each other and having fun in each other's company. In the future you will all become better photographers making awesome images.

This way of giving and sharing is more important than you might think when you initially reflect on this. I've spent a lot of time in the world of judo, where there are no "secret" techniques. Even "new" applications of a techniques used in some tournament were swiftly transferred into the judo community through local instructors and practicing.

In a similar way it is possible to share your knowledge within the photographic community. It is not through keeping a "secret" method to yourself that you will grow as a person / photographer. It is rather through sharing and practicing with other people. All the ideas that you choose to work with, and the picks you make from the palette of photographic possibilities and use to work with is your choice. That goes for the possible "fads" too. If you can do some nice images with the aid of a black plastic bag, then share that knowledge. There will be other pieces of knowledge coming back to you expanding your knowledge. Guarding "secrets" means more work than it is worth. You will probably spend more time and effort hiding how you work, rather than using it and letting other people in on the technique you apply to your images. There is nothing threatening in that, at all, since photography, or art in general, is not about what techniques you use. It is rather more about if the viewer will get something out of looking at your images, or not. Does your image have something to say? Does it really provoke sensations in the minds of people looking at it? That is, are there enough common denominators to catch the interest of the viewer.

What are my arguments for discussing this? Simply speaking, don't waste your effort and time on "gruelling" stuff that does not need to be kept secret, since those "secrets" are probably already known out there, and half of your photographing friends probably use them, thinking nothing of it. You're just wasting your energy in keeping on doing this "secret" move. Spend your energy on your photography and less of it with being troubled over stuff that does not matter.

Then you will be able to spend time making images. That's supposed to be your main interest and not all that stuff that comes along with owning some camera equipment. You will not be interested in wasting your time. You should first and foremost be interested in making photographic images, and maybe even show them to people around you. Then you are, perhaps, making a difference. Don't create "wars" with fellow photographers about stuff that is in no way as important as making new images. That time consuming "sport" is not fitting for someone trying to capture the time around us. Your main driving force ought to be to make as many good, or even amazing, images as you're capable of during your life. That's your main objective. Save the time spent arguing for your images – let them argue, low affectively, for you! If you're not there yet – keep on making images the best you can, until you feel bold enough to show them to others.

Okay, so the methods you will apply – do they have anything to do with the "photographs" that you create? If you're able to compose a well-rounded "complicated" image thanks to some "luck" when doing it in a not obviously "conscious" manner, you ought to be able to recreate that image, thinking about all odds and ends that will go into it to make it a "simple", yet "complicated" image, with some "story" or "riddle" built into it. How you are thinking when doing that is hardly any secret, is it? Let me give you, at least, two answers to that question.

Firstly, if that hack makes it possible for you to earn money and no one else is capable of duplicating your hack. Then go ahead, try making money on it!

Secondly, if it is more than probable that several bright individuals within the upcoming week will have duplicated your hack, then it's not worth the hassle trying to keep it a secret anymore. You don't have to tell anyone how it is done, but you don't have to go at length trying to cover it up either. Simply let it be – use it – and if anyone is interested, tell that person how you do it. It's nothing more to it. That road is easier to follow than trying to keep it a secret. You want to make images, not to be a guardian of secrets.

You will find, when you let go of your idea that your secrets have to be kept secret at all costs, that your life is becoming much more easy to live. You may concentrate on your image making and planning of future images you want to make, instead of guarding a "hack" that anyone with a bit of luck and a receptive mind is capable of coming up with.

So, return to your image making, to your cameras and the rays of light that make photography possible in the first place. You must watch yourself, so you don't fall into that kind of paralyzing traps from time to another. That is probably the most important decision you have made in a very, very long time. It's all about trying to harness the skills and the will to attain the goals of making awesome images, not getting lost in a way that don't help you to reach those goals. Then you will have all the time you need to make those amazing images you are longing to execute, but you keep yourself from doing.

The stuff that may become an obstacle is not good for you – you must stop letting yourself getting stuck on stuff like that. There is not enough time to have a lot of issues like that in your life. Instead of guarding, start showing and you will find that your healthy colleagues will, in turn, share their work with you. There will, discouragingly so, always be some people that don't share. But you don't have to be too friendly with them, do you? It's all too easy to become a victim of circumstances, and we don't want any of that, do we? You probably have your goals in becoming a master of your photographic endeavors and that means that you don't have time, nor endurance, enough to spend it on stuff that in essence make you execute those since long overdue images that you have dreamt about for ages. You don't seem to have the time and you don't seem to have the endurance to cope with all the stuff following concepts like that – you should be out there, in reality, making images out of it! Hopefully images that transcend reality when you show those pictures.

The stuff that you engage in will be the things that you are concentrating on. If you're engaged and NOT telling anybody about your activities then that manner of reaching out and not acting out will be what you are becoming good at. Since you engage in that activity you will take time away from your photography and thus, will not become any better or, worse, will never be able to make those awesome images you always dream of making.

That means that your idea about photography is shovel into the background, while you are stuck with coping with hiding the basic level hack you have stumbled upon. The times you spend with other things when you really have set this time aside in order to spend it making images, will be a near total waste. You cannot blame anybody but yourself for this. You have chosen the manner you act accordingly to. Will there ever be a different way to deal with this? Maybe there is, but, don't concentrate all your hopes in that this will happen. Set your course for your action and stick to it. Allow no deviations!

You totally own your objectives, so you're responsible for reaching them. You're even responsible for the time it takes and the money you spend on it. Does that indicate that you may use any positive reactions for your benefit too? Yes, it does! Since you own you project you will own even all the negative stuff it generates. I might add that in general it accounts for all reactions that you might stir with your images. All the stuff you let into your project has to be scanned for its usability, otherwise you might incorporate some really bad stuff. This might stop you from any progress and, it probably will make you low.

That's why I argue that all that unnecessary stuff must go, you don't have to engage in all that waste of time, it is definitely not in your best interests for your future work with your images. It's a no go area of activity. It is wisest for you not to get into that area. We might even call it a forbidden zone. You had better stay away! Your life will become so much easier if you manage to discipline yourself. If you try to sort out what you decide if you were going to make at least one awesome image, or if the possibilities of that will stay at zero level regarding your chances for the rest of your life.

If the dream of some of your goals is set by others, how is it then possible for you to reach them? All the arguments that disagree with your own ideas are irrelevant arguments. You have a certain amount of time at your disposal for your photography depending on if you have a family, what kind of profession you work within and what kind of other interests you have. So, let's ague that you have five (5) hours per week to spend on photography. All the time is taken away from your five hours not making photography is counterproductive. That disappearing time does not lead you towards more and better photography. Okay, are you with me? Everything that takes time away from your allotted five hours are bad. Of course, that time maybe have to be moved around in your schedule, since your family and work always must be priority number one. Watching sports, or movies on television, is not. If that watching is not a part of a plan to scout for ways of making interesting images. So, simply don't waste your time set aside for photography!

If you're watching sports to learn more about neat angles to use when you're out there shooting images, so be it! If you're watching a movie with some photographic plot, so be it! Everything else is a waste of your time when it comes to your development as a photographer. If you're serious in your endeavors, that means that you have to have your objectives clearly in sight. You're not allowed to lose your target!

The more single minded you succeed in becoming, the better! It does not have to be only hardships; it is possible to bend anything to become a part of your photographic development. You just have to look at the activities in a different manner. What is one thing may also become several things. That is, watching your kids play soccer might be an exercise in making soccer images. But, don't forget to really watch your kid and be able to discuss the match with her afterwards! You may make some images during the match, but remember that it is not your main reason for being there. The main reason is to watch YOUR kid playing soccer. Don't forget that!

You may handle the rest of your life with ease. Making images while you're living your life. Don't let the photographing become the main activity. You are probably not in this world to make photography only!

The time you spend watching your kid playing soccer are nice, so cherish them and really watch your kid growing up with your full attention! You don't want to hear twenty years from now that: "you were always making images of the other kids playing"!

In the same vein – don't let your job results grew bad because of your photography. You always have to earn money and some days you don't have to make images! Your income is important as an enabler of your photographic ventures. Don't rely on earning money on your photographic venture before you really have some regular assignments. Wishing is one thing – reality is another. You have to pay your rent, pay for your food, so, don't miss out on your work!

The ambitions you have incorporated into your daily living must be about living up to your role as a parent and a provider. If you're going into the uncertain realm of pro-photography you have to have your family being in on it. They should not have to pay for you trying suddenly to live your dream. Your family has the right to be informed on your new ambitions.

Since you are a serious person you won't let things like that happen, will you? Do your thing! Try to earn money, but don't leave your day job until you have some revenue from your photography. You will have to come to terms with the perspective that becoming a pro-photographer will mean that you might experience that doing your most favorite thing is not as nice as when you do it all by yourself.

When you are a pro you will have to meet customers that want you to realize their ideas. You can set your mark on the images, but if the customer wants the color red in all the images, you had better see to it that there is red in all the images. That is the ways commission goes. As a pro you have to see to it that your customers are satisfied, or they will not return. In this case, your new day time job is no longer a job, but returning to being a mere hobby. You'll have to find an opening in the trade you were employed in earlier. That's the way the shutter closes.

Okay, some make it as photographers – but remember that most don't. Even photographers that has made a name for themselves are struggling with teaching photography, making books, holding exhibitions, or applying for grants to survive. The biggest obstacle is the important issue about getting paid for your services. So, maybe you should make a list, or even a couple of lists, of what you willing to do in order to make it as a photographer. There are possibilities to pursue. Within the real estate business there is a constant demand for photographic services, as do people getting married, and to some extent making class photos in schools. These three branches will perhaps not pay your rent. They are commissions, with certain rules, that you must follow in order to be contacted again. Either you contact some players in the field, or you try starting your own business within those fields.

In this part some things like how to make time for your photographic endeavors have been discussed. Some of the main features discussed above are:

- don't grow too single minded, spend time with your family
- scout for new areas of photographic interest
- don't lose your day job

Where to Sell Images

There are several large Internet based agencies, like Shutterstock and the like in the high end, craving rather technically demanding images, and reasonable kickbacks, down to agencies like Mostphotos with very simple, matter-of-fact images with captions like door, field, clouds etc. that don't pay that much for each of your images they sell. At agencies like Mostphotos you must sell in great bulk to get hold of serious money.

There are Internet agencies who cater to the PR-business, where you may make serious bucks selling sunsets, diving images, pictures from nature and so on. There seems to be possibilities to sell images of interior design, but I reckon that the guys already in that sector may have a finger in that game, and access to a lot of homes to make images of.

The real positive thing with the image agencies is that are alive 24/seven, and real sales of your images is a question of how close you are to the mainstream ideals in any given industry. You really don't have to be well connected, or a good sales person.

If you are considering printing and framing your images and selling them in that format yourself it will work if you don't sell that much. But, when, and if, you start selling more, there will also be more work for you, meaning that you limit the time you ought to spend making new images. You'll be occupied printing, framing, packaging and sending the images off. There are agencies that will do that for you too! Thus, they are freeing you to keep on doing more images.

Let's be honest, it will take time before you will survive selling a picture a month! Eventually it will probably be about selling five to ten images per day, all the 30 days of the month and that is a lot of printing, framing and packaging you have to do to pay your rent. You have to ponder if you want to make yourself into an image-factory, or if you want to go on making images. The risk you're taking is that you will get stuck in that genre, whether you like it, or not. So, have your sentiments about making images from start to finish diminished after making your 350th print and framing in one week? You have suddenly been transformed into a one-trick-pony! Was it really that you wished for being on your agenda earlier? Finding your niche is also about cutting yourself off from possible dabbling in other fields. If you have occasional jumping days that may be okay, but watch out for it to becoming a habit.

The more in demand any of your skills become, the less the rest of your skills will be in demand. Pity then if your own favorites are the ones in lesser demand. That is how working life is, you're selling your skills and not all of your skills are in high demand all of the time. Not all of your dogs are really jumping at the same time.

But really; it's all photography, isn't it? I made my living for almost four decades mostly handling texts; writing, editing, proofing, doing layout, making some of the images, you name it. Maybe I had dreams about something more specialized, but all the ways you can treat texts are in a way a constant challenge which means that you learn something new, almost every working day. I even think there is a lot about of transferring, like, for example, when editing other writer's texts you pick up stuff now and then that over time make you a better writer. Even when others proofread your texts it is time and again something to be learnt by their comments. I am talking about colleagues that was driven in handling the language – above the "hunch level". In a way in the same realm with images, some texts are better when they are "fast and furious", rather than "dull and slow" – all depending on what their purpose is. So, in a manner you will get more like a pro when you get used to handle vast amounts of photographic images supposed to live up to some hard core specifications – like that there has to appear something "red" in every frame, or "need to have a soft blue sky at the top. All this since your customer wants it that way. Then there might be "punctum" that is even might be more important than the "red", or the "blue sky".

Why can this become some nuisance – or problem? Your problems surface when you think that any commissioned images always will be yours to decide how they should look or be manipulated. Some of your customers don't want your "mark" on these images, since they didn't pick you to make them because they like your "style". They choose you because you were available with a reasonable price tag. Possibly they think you know what you are doing. Every image that you may upload at these Internet agencies do not have to be, or cannot be, 'art'. The images have to be technically good images. Since you make them to support yourself when making your 'own' images, they have to be done swiftly, so you may have time to spend making your 'own' images.

Even if work is part of living – only "work" is not living. You have to make room for your own photography. Even bringing an extra camera to the shots you're commissioned to do, in order to make room for your own photography, might be a way of getting the most out of the situation. If you do commissioned work with your own camera, just shoot your extra work 'on the run' during the commissioned shoot.

In this part some things like selling your images have been discussed. One of the main features discussed above is:

- Internet agencies for image commerce

The Rigging of Life

Previously we have discussed the rigging of your life to make it possible for you to earn your living by photography or, at least supplement your income selling images for publication. There are some pro's and con's when arranging your life in order to be able to do that.

Firstly there are of course pros like that you, within your business, will be in possession of equipment that you have access to and may use when you're out making your more personal images.

Secondly, you might through your commissions be let in at places, or locations, that you would have trouble entering on your own. That opens up opportunities for your more 'artistic' work, using the locations you encounter on commissions.

Thirdly, you might become a better photographer, since you practice a lot. And presumedly understand how to incorporate your new findings into your repertoire.

On the downside there are stuff that mostly is about that you may lose track of your original concepts about what kind of photography you want to do. So, you have to remind yourself all the time that you're on a mission – not only to earn a living, but, ultimately, in order to make some awesome images.

You have to avoid becoming caught up in the details of your commissions. Okay, you have to deliver more than acceptable material, but remember that this is not what you're expected to fret over at midnight.

The manner that you express yourself photographically may shift over time. That does not necessarily indicate a bad thing. Change may be both good and bad. Try to see to it that you benefit from all eventual change making you a better photographer. In the long run you will not make all pictures looking great, but that should become your goal. "No images below par!" The images in your life will over time become a life-long love affair, based on the effort you put in creating them. So, even if your 100 best images were exposed at 1/250 second, together they may be argued to categorize what you did during five decades. I think that it is the long run that counts.

Some famous photographers may have made a couple of houndreds of amazing images, but they share a portfolio of 50 images that they themselves regard as awesome. That means that they have had a consistency in their work that runs over decades and transcends all "memes" and what is on the agenda during a very limited time. Consistency is about keeping your standard at as high level as possible. It's about keeping up with your best images at least a couple of times per year to increase the portfolio of your stunning images per annum.

Consistency might be argued to be the basics of any skill — it is what separates the craftsman from the beginner. The craftsman has some strategies to get to grips with a certain photo-session. He does not have to do the guess-work like a novice. The craftsman has discovered the traps in any given image … the light ray passing from left to right, the shadows rising to grow into yet another dark space in the image. The novice does not observe these dangers and is heading for a corrupt image that no image processing software may save – at least as you probably are a novice handling that kind of software too. So, the more experienced photographer is given a head start all the time he is aiming, or just glancing, at something.

But, don't despair, there's hope. The novice will eventually pick up on the things he has to know to be able to aim for consistency. It will probably be a sudden realization; 'I know how to handle this', rather than an elaborate development with a conscious emotion of getting more skilled. No matter how skilled you think you are, you can always freshen up a bit on any of the small parts of your sets of skills.

That's a very comforting thought, it means that even the phantoms and the sorcerers of any trade may improve their performance. Perhaps not in any significantly giant steps, but there's always room for getting more accomplished. It's a humbling experience to grasp the thought that someone you admire in any given field may become even more admirable, given that they improve their skills.

One thing about skills, or knowledge: my mum used to state: "knowledge is no burden". I still think that it is very sound advice. You cannot know too much! There is no such thing!

So, you don't even have to choose what to learn next. That piece you just learnt will come in handy anywhere in your life, you just wait and see! Look upon it as an investment – all the small things you pick up are together, or, will together result in something else – much bigger than you could have anticipated. That means that you too will emerge like somebody better and more adapted after you have acquired that knowledge.

That will be a different you – maybe even a very much improved version of you. The most meriting thing about it is that you have done it all by yourself. You have acquired all that knowledge and will perhaps know how to make the best use of it. Then you have become a contender on the photographic market within the photographic industry. That is good if that's where you want to be, but if you spent a lot of time with photography you've probably already gotten some rewards, simply being there, doing that. This is regardless of if you have earned any money doing it. Maybe photography is what you really want to spend your time doing, and again, maybe not? Let's be clear about that when you go professional, there is not any longer any possibility to "hope" for your images ending up okay. They have to be okay, or you'll soon find out that you'll stop receiving phone calls about assignments. When your photography is a hobby you may spend all of your photographing just hanging around. Not the case when people commission you to do make images at an event, or the like. They expect that you deliver, there's no way around that. You have to deliver what you promised, not anything else. That special "anything else" you may offer as "the icing on the cake", to be rejected, or accepted, not like the images you were expected to shoot.

That is the main difference between being an amateur and being a professional photographer. You've better learn that, or be made aware of it at a much later stage in your career. That is the way the 'cookie crumbles', like they said. You are the creator of your images and you are the creator of your fortune too. That is depending on how you deal with the assignments you are now scouting for. So, the fortune ahead of you is yours to be captured, you decide how you will go about that.

The reason you should man up into being that serious that you are able to is that you have to get an air about you that reeks of seriousness. You may be fun to work with, but you must have intense confidence in your customers. See to it that you have that, or they will not return back to you to let you have another go. I guess it's all about trust. If they trust you to deliver what's been agreed upon, then they'll return to you for your next assignment. If they are insecure about your abilities in any way, they won't. There is no way around that. You have to institute trust, or you have to give up photography as a professional vocation. So, how hard can it be?

You may talk about the "stories" in your images at length, but if the viewers don't "see" your "stories" you're not using any kind of universal stories, but rather only stories that are in your head. As long as they remain there, they will not transcend the distance over to other people's minds. They will appear rather lame, existing only in your mind, being only a construct of your way of thinking. You have to create a 'door' into your 'story', making it possible for any viewer to grasp.

Think about why you do what used to be called "snap shots" (fast decision photography). These shots are made because your eyes see something before your brain has the possibility to grasp what caught your attention. When you looked at your images, there were a lot of images that resembled each other, but sometimes there was some exiting ones. Even you had to admit that.

That's the "story" you must try to catch, it's always there, if only you come close enough and don't evaluate the images before making them. Your brain might be pressing you into some directions. Trust that emotion and go for those images – some will be crap – but some will be worth gold, or at least silver. No, you cannot make that happen all the time, but you will soon make really good images if you trust your instinct – not only your eyes.

When you're trying to become better at what you do, you might ask yourself if that is something that comes from within, or is it about stuff that others impose on you, thinking it is good for you to know? There are some differences between those two that you need to know how to do all this stuff by yourself. You want to learn that stuff and that is a major difference. You may not want to acquire that knowledge, that is exposed to you by others. It's what others want you to know. That may not be in your best interest.

The choice of what to learn must come from within you, otherwise it is useless and without the drive to make you endure the hardships it will mean to learn that new stuff. The importance of your inner drive cannot be exaggerated enough. You might make minor improvements at the request of someone else, but for you to make major changes you must really want to learn, be taught, or whatever all the things you learn must be chosen by you, made by you and done by you. You must be the one stress-sing yourself to the rim of exhaustion to make that knowledge stick.

The most obvious way to get hold of that way of learning your trade is to lean back and enjoy the ride along the road into the future of better photography, better images and perhaps, a better attitude towards photography.

The chase for better images and a raised level of skill will, in the best of worlds, result in an improved attitude towards what an image really is. When you start to look upon your images as something to wrestle with, to talk to in order to have their stories revealed to you, that's when you are starting to create images.

The knowledge will seep into you, like through osmosis, you will gradually get more and better accomplished as a photographer. That means that you in a way will become a stranger, or at least, another person than the one you once were. This will happen because you will gradually adapt a different view on the world surrounding you. In a manner of speaking, you will become a person who you were not earlier. Of course, you will not be totally transformed from top to bottom, but you will value images more intensively than before, and you will become a person that you earlier in your life would have regarded as a stranger, 'the other', in the anthropological sense, someone who differs from your earlier being.

Whatever that signifies it means an important change, or not. It's up to you to decide what that means. If you notice that your images are becoming influenced by your newly acquired skills remains to be seen in the future. Remember; it is hard to become 'better' if you don't define what that improvement should include, and how you are going to measure it. Maybe it is better to think of your progress as 'change'. Do your images become different in any significant way or, could you argue that they have become different over time? If so, they might be on their path of becoming better too.

Since 'better' is an evaluation, or grading, you have to decide what images by other photographers your material should be compared to. Try to create a starting level that indicates your 'zero level'. Compare your work with that image, or set of images. Do your discover change? What kind of change are we talking about here? Is it possible to use the word 'different' about it? Or, even the word 'improvement'? Are you leaving 'status quo' on your way along the path of development, or is it only that you apply technicalities like new filters and new lenses?

The use of new technical stuff does not necessarily mean that your images are becoming 'better'. You might call them more technically advanced, but content wise you are in for the surprise that technicalities are only going to result in effects on the surface of your images. You want to go deep into the guts of your images, don't you?

You want to become a 'deep image diver', you want to venture below the surface of your images – dealing with the complex psychological action that is going on when we study an image. Your quest is to enter below the surface into the realm of what constitutes an image. Reaching into the very 'essence' of images you will become able to shape that 'soul' as you go along.

W.J.T. Mitchell argues that images possess 'agency', and in order to get under their skin when regarding them, we must take that in consideration. The images possess a force that may establish influences on the viewer. If Mitchell is right, maybe it's possible to enter the realm behind the surface of the images and, on our behalf load them with 'meaning' for lack of a better word. Since most attempts in filling images with some kind of 'meaning' in a way have to rely on a common way of looking upon the world, sometimes regardless of how the 'culture' we happen to live within is looked upon as 'ours'. This has a lot to do with how we look upon images. Maybe it is really the viewers who are filled with 'meaning' and they are transferring that concept into the images they are looking at. That will mean that images either are filled with some kind of 'meaning' or, the spectators are the ones that supply the 'meaning'.

Are human objects being influenced, not by the 'content' of the image. But rather being manipulated by their own ideas about 'content'? Thus the images work as some kind of 'triggers' – and in every initiative of the thought of that content. We are here talking about what lies below the surface of the images.

Different individuals may think an image is 'good' for a lot of different reasons. "It reminds me of my grandmother!", "Just the way I remember London", or "I once lived in a house on that street", or "It is important to focus on stuff like that" — and those persons are referring to the same image! So, the value driven directions concerning 'good' or 'bad' are really a nest of problems, to say the least!

During the work of creeping below the surface of your images it might be easier if you visualize the image, or on the object, that has more depth and weight than an okay print out — or a file on one of your hard drives.

In short, you could put the question like; does the image have agency and leave traces like it really is some kind of being? Would there be anything missed if we erase these images from our lives? Given that humans are constructed as highly visually wired and trained, with an inborn capacity to handle different kinds of images, pictograms and symbols, would we miss images if they no longer existed? It is of course really hard to imagine a future life where there no longer is anything with even the slightest resemblance of what we normally call an image, since an image is a highly coded way of communication.

Many objects in our natural world react, for example, if you bend a twig on a tree it might break, or bounce right back when you let go of it. In the ordinary case the twig does not 'act' on its own. It is just a twig, swinging gently in the breeze, it does not, we presume, have a will of its own, but it co-plays in our lives, so, it might be said to encompass some kind of agency, even if it is not based on the twigs having a 'free will' and ideas about what it will partake in.

In that sense it reminds us of the situation of images. They don't really interact with the viewer, but rather trigger reactions in the viewer. Like I wrote earlier, my main view on this is that the spectator has memories, emotions or, combinations of them that trigger a new set of reminiscences and, the viewer feels, or thinks, that this is coming out of the image, speaking to her. The image in itself might be looked upon as a piece of dead matter. As far as we know today, or assume, dead matter does not act. So, is there a point where I can cook you an image as dead matter?

If the concept of 'agency', when we assume that things are agents in our lives holds true, we have to change the way we look upon "things" in general. They might appear to be just 'dead' matter now, because we have not a really good way of describing them in any other way. We cannot fathom the idea that "things" partake in our lives in an active manner. Nature may be "alive", but an image may only be argued to "exist". The games the photographs may be said to play with our emotions are a part of a far bigger scheme than just "living" or, "existing". Both "nature" and "things" may be argued to require space in the physical world. Humankind is of course a part of the "nature". The way we go about treating our relations with the two entities are really an example of difference in kind. On the one side we have the natural world (the earth without mankind, to put it simple) and on the other hand we find all the things man has constructed, like houses, railroads, books, and, of course, cameras! By the more extremist views on this you might look at images as if they were souvenirs from the real world, when you regard them, you're just looking at someone's memory, mixing it up with your own memories and finding av story hidden in them.

If a photograph is the result of man trying to copy, alter, or enhance nature we are in the similar realm as fiction writing. It's built on the world as it is, you adapt, or change, some of the stuff in it, and, all of a sudden, you have created a totally novel world. An image is in its essence the makings of an individual, but that individual is a mixture of ideas from hundreds or, thousands of other human beings. So, is it that heritage that sips through the surface of an individual photographic image?

Is it the things appearing in a photography that affects us, really part of the heritage in the same manner that ancient sound recordings making it possible to listen to the actual voices of individuals born almost 200 years ago? If they speak at a time, long ago we might notice their special accent, the way they use concepts since long not in use anymore.

Photography plays some kind of similar role, it might make us remember, showing us novel points of view or, just stating the fact; once upon a time this tennis ball laid on my breakfast table. The image ends up in our heads — together with all of the similar images we have ever seen. One thing new images might do is to bring us back in time, make us think about things we thought we had forgotten, etc. Some kind of time travel, if you wish.

The manner in which the images transcends all of our defenses towards outer stimulation is in itself a fascinating trait. We don't seem to have any real defense towards images, seen in retrospect we might argue "this cannot be", or, something to that effect. We are nevertheless vulnerable when exposed to images. It seems evolution got the best of us and reason has very little to do with how we react. It is like the images attack us when our guards are down. Thus, we will always be affected in the worst of degrees — we will become victims of circumstances. In this case it is all about emotions rising within us and overpowering our inner existence.

That sounds so threatening that it almost implies that images maybe should be banned? Does that mean that the photography really does not exist until someone sees it and is affected by its agencies? Does the image not exist when the photographer is done with it? It seems like the old question: "If a tree falls in the deep of the forest and nobody watches it falling, has it really fallen?" When we speak about photography, the image has at least been seen by the photographer, but she doesn't see it like the upcoming viewer, she is involved in this image, maybe even the image is a portal to the photographer in a way it never can be a portal opening up the road to the inner life of the viewer? But, since I agree that what we "see" in an image partly already is situated within us as viewers, it is not really adequate to talk too much about the stories within the images we regard. The story is partly, or, for the major part already within our heads.

So, we will regard images differently depending on whatever we are the creators of the image or, an unsuspecting spectator? One thing is for sure, and that is that the two are approaching the image from different angles. The differences between the two will decide whatever they are touched by the magic in the image in front of them. Does it mean that we never may look at an image the same way? Different persons looking will probably look at the image differently. The same image being studied at two different moments in time? Will this suffice to create different experiences?

Why am I going on about this? Is there really a problem? I would not really call it a problem, but these are interesting questions, at least in my world, and they lead towards the idea that experiences may differ, and they will differ wildly, since nothing is given about what is the right way to react to, or interpret, an image. The way we must react is not given, there is no need for consensus about what that image tells us. "This image is about …" is not an option. The truth is that people do not have to 'understand' an image in any given way. There are no fixed interpretations. Those who claim that are in a way just very pretentious and trying to put you down for not being able to give the 'right' answers.

We shall not dwell that long on what is 'right or wrong', let's think about them as 'alternative interpretations'!

I will concentrate my writing on the things I find strange in the interpretations of images. The main reason is really that among some amateur photographers there are ideas within academic writing about photography indicating that scholars don't even understand what an image is. Given that there is some evidence of that kind of scholarly writing, there is perhaps a rather wide discrepancy between the way 'ordinary' people regard images and the way scholars handle them. For good, or for worse, it is not my aim to dissect that here. I will touch upon the dichotomy here and there.

Even if I mention other kinds of images the main scoop in this text is about photographic images. This is mainly a result of my interest in photography. All kinds of images may be said to be related, so even if I try concentrating on photographic images, you will find that my arguments also includes other kinds of images, like paintings, symbols or, iconography at large. I often mention them in order to support my arguments about photography. One reason for that is that I reckon that people who have not made a painting may have done some photographs. So, trying to keep my arguments mainly about photography I hope for a clearer understanding of my text.

One additional thought borders within the ongoing discussion on digital imagery as distinct from analog imagery. The arguments in this discussion are mainly based on the digitals photography's possibility to make vast amounts of images at a low price. There are literally no economic limitations to make images with these tools. I will not go into the differences here (those interested may check out my book EMBALMED TIME : Photography in the Post Photographic Era, 2020).

One of the major problems with distilling one's strengths is that the thoughts in a way come in clusters, where it might be hard to distinguish what is the cause, and what appears to be the effect. What is a "normal" image, compared to all the "non normal" images? It is hard to distinguish between them, but I'll try making my best effort.

The time you spend trying to figure out how images are connecting may not have any impact on the images you make yourself. Still, you will perhaps get an inkling of the idea of what kind of images you're interested in. The ones you make yourself does not need to have anything in common with the images you prefer to study or, just like to look at in art galleries, and the like.

The images you like yourself play an integral part in your photographic life as a 'consumer' of images. I'm fond of van Gogh, Gauguin, Goya, some street photographers like Doisneau and so on. The list is really infinite. I doubt that I measure other images I see with these all the time. Okay, it might happen on occasion that I make a reference to other photographers, or painters with a comment like: "This is very Edward Hopperish!" or, "This is so Dalí!". Does this indicate that the eventual heritage from these artists does carry on into my own material?

Imagine that it is the opposite. Who wants to make images that are "like" someone else's? That indicates that you're making some kind of mainstream images, that in a sense are 'replicas' of somebody's images. Who wants to do that, and who wants to be mainstream? Of course, mainstream is good if you want revenue. Mainstream images sell, like sunsets or lighthouse in a storm. I like to aim outside of mainstream, trying to make images that don't please the eye or mind, but rather irritates, or points towards alternative framing of the 'reality' that creates the basis of my images.

I generally erase, or at least don't show anyone, the images I figure are looking like a 'Doisneau', or the like, since that image has already been made, and I don't have to be the one repeating just that image. I might have learnt some things doing the replicant image, but is not really "mine". I might put in into an album called 'paraphrasing'. When you have done that image you know how to make it, so you don't have to repeat it, ever again.

Maybe all the things that we have to learn are meant to be hard to get in order for us to appreciate them when we have mastered them? Otherwise I would not be much point in making a difference between the one who possess the skill and the other one, who doesn't, would there? The new things we apprehend might be the things we, after some time, become most comfortable with and sometimes it's hard to "unlearn" bad habits. It's like, if you know how to ride a bicycle, it is very hard to "unlearn" that skill to the extent that you would fall sideways trying to ride a bike. Even a language you know well enough to read novels, or even poetry in, may evolve as a passable spoken voice given the proper time and circumstances. You might not have tried to speak that language in twenty years, but it is still there, somewhere in your head, rusty at the start, but fully functional after a couple of days in the right setting.

I mean that it is in a way similar to our human vision, if we don't constantly "hunt" for details in our environment, but given a camera we will suddenly see that stuff again if we are out there again tracking down images. Our "skills" have never abandoned us, really have just made a pause in their activity, they are not lost, only somewhat neglected over time.

The way we change direction of our interests at certain points in time seems to be mostly dependent on chance. Circumstances force us to avoid or, abort, some manners of expression and temporarily give up some preferences. We just dull them down for some time, busying us with stuff that mainly is related with the things we left. In that way we are very single-minded, what seems to be a wide field of interests is really a very well niched compartment of things to do. In that "box", if you like, we alter very little over time. Basically because we are rather consistent over time, we rarely cultivate very extraordinary "likes", they are rather spin-offs from stuff we have favorized for quite some time already. There will really be no surprise there, rather the other way around, in that sense we are very predictable.

That is not necessarily something bad, or good

either for that matter. It rather points towards that we are deeply set in our ways and that it will take some time to come up with totally new ideas, or concepts. We seem rather to tend to develop existing interests and hobbies in new directions, rather than venturing into something totally fresh.

Maybe we spend time at 'natural' development, or 'the route of interests', pointing us towards new variations of an already familiar track. Rather than getting forced to entirely new equipment, or gear, we make use of what we already own, and use our gear in new combinations.

So, you may call it development, getting along on the beaten track of life with a controlled number of surprises. Some of it new stuff, but mostly well known.

This may be the result of a completely natural development – you start at one point, and then move to another. You stop there for a while and then you proceed to yet another point along a road you don't have covered by a map. It might feel like you venture into a hostile and strange environment, but you have to go there. There is no other option if you want to learn, and advance, your skills.

One step at a time – you will get some place in the vicinity of places you have already been. Not too scary, you might get there without too many surprises.

So, it's safe to change, or develop, in stages, not going all the from A to Z, but rather pause at B, C, D, and so on. Perhaps you will experience progress, not really changing much with each step. Nothing is scary – it might feel uncomfortable – yet, everything is safe!

In this part some things like ‘stories’ have been discussed. One of the main features discussed above is:

• The importance of loading your images with content giving the viewer a ’handle’ to your ‘story’.

Approaching ideas

The best way to introduce yourself to new ideas is to approach them as something you shouldn't go near. In a way, like something forbidden. That will awaken your curiosity, like for most of us. That does not mean that it has to be experienced as a bad approach. With curiosity you will be capable of getting close to the subjects, or areas, your really not interested in, and to your surprise you might discover that this is some kind of interesting stuff.

That is possibly the case since you have a lot to learn by approaching subjects that have not yet caught your interest.

The possibility that you will become interested when you abandon all, or, almost all, of your favorite ways to come closer to areas that you are not already familiar with, will help lower the barriers you have raised against these specific topics. When approaching them in a different manner does lower your defenses and may probably let you enjoy the new knowledge you will be acquiring.

That will probably enable you to disregard your hang-ups about certain topics and move on to include them in your world of photography and will, for sure, broaden your perspective on what photography may, and, possibly could be. That, my friend, might be that giant step forward in your development as a photographer, maybe indicating a new direction, or not. You will have to embrace this new outlook for a while to get accustomed to it.

It is important that you have an open mind about change. Getting at close range of new ideas, you will perhaps shy away, or at least, hopefully, take to it in a new manner.

One major idea is to not shy away from stuff you haven't dealt with earlier, but rather take it in, try it, and maybe open your heart to it. I promise, it's lots of interesting stuff you haven't tried out yet that is really worth trying out. If you really don't like it, you may discard it later on. There's really no hurry, the topics will still be there when you've become ready to fathom them at you own good pace.

The time you spend running away from new, or rather, unused ideas, will not let you develop in a good way. You might think that you are zooming in to become a specialist? How do you know what your special area of expertise is? Is it what you are already interested in, or something else, you want to gain some expertise in? Whatever your answer is, remember that if it easy, it is probably not worth it. The motifs you haven't tried yet, for whatever reason, might be the ones that are waiting for you.

So, when deciding whether you should try something new, always go for what is new! Always try the stuff that pops up in your head, there is probably good grounds for it to do that popping. You might want to try that before you die!

The way you go for these ideas you want to incorporate in your repertoire is, of course, up to you. You will always have the chance to make that knowledge a part of your skill set. It is never too late to get wise in that new area. You will get a broader sense for your photography, and that might lead you into new ideas on how to get going in all sorts of new directions.

The ideas that we strive to experience are the ones that we might enjoy, as well. It doesn't take too long to experience something new – at least that that is the rule, it seems. You probably do enjoy your exercises in a deeper quality when you have spent more time with them, getting comfortable with them, and don't spend all the time with doing stuff that you have been doing for the last 40 years. When making efforts to encompass new areas you will experience mot fatigue than usual, but that is just your system adjusting to these new concepts to are trying to get to grips with. If you study the gaze of a boxer, or a soccer player, you'll notice the glare of concentration manifesting itself in the eyes.

How you'll get yourself into that realm of concentration is entirely up to you. There will be an appendix with some tips at the end of this book.

So, concentration is a key ingredient in any vocation, even so photography. You scan your surroundings, keep an eye upon what is happening, have an eye open to identify the possibly "good" spots of interest and just wait for something to happen. This is what I think about as "set scenes", much alike the big game shooting of exotic animals in fenced in areas. Not much of a sport, really. But, sports event events like soccer games, football games, wrestling or boxing is a whole other ballpark. There will be something happening there. Take your time learning the rules of the games. If you really understand this game, you're trying to make images of, you will have a much smoother ride. You will be able to anticipate moves and be ready for them. Your choice now is trying to identify what is going to happen on a whole lot more detailed level. Try to think ahead, there might at least be three possible turns the development may go at any given moment of the game. Try to for see obstacles like security guards, the sound guy, and/or the film-crew at the event.

Don't wait until the last minute to check your gear. Check it and test your equipment with some frames. You'll be glad that you did this in advance, you'll be ahead of your own planning that way.

The time you spend preparing is well spent, you will be glad later, when you discover that the traits you scouted will work and that some of them will not work, at all.

Then, you have the choice to adapt to the alternatives you figured out due to your early preparations. You're prepared, and will be better at ease for it. All that preparation will mean (in the ideal case) that the unplanned stuff will benefit from what you catch during your outing. You will probably sense an acute awareness of the limitations that you are experiencing. In the case that planning ruins your shots, please let me know (there is an email address at the end of this book). I'm eagerly waiting to hear from you.

When you're all set to go, you only have to wait for the show to begin. Remember to work systematically – shooting surroundings, atmosphere and then, the actual performance! In the case of a recess, check what you have caught on your memory card, and make a mental note to yourself about you think you are still missing. After the intermission you start filling in the gaps in you story. Then, start concentrating on what you want to expand, shots of the artists in action, close ups on instrument and props, or whatever. Think about your photo shoot as a box of chocolate that you are filling up with your images. It might be a box containing only close ups, or it might be a varied box of confiture if you try to cover the entire event.

Whatever road you choose to concentrate on the stuff you set out to catch will be different, if you have a more open mind. There will surface opportunities that you had never been able to foresee, now you just have to go for them. You have no master plan, trying to fulfill that. It doesn't mean that you should close your eyes to the unexpected. You know as well as I, that in this lies many opportunities. Do your homework, but take care of the freebies! There may be images to be remembered surfacing all around you!

So, plan for the expected, but be prepared for the unexpected too! Be a boy scout of photography; be prepared! It almost goes without saying that you always should be open to new opportunities and jump at them whenever they appear in your path. That means, in principle, that your focus never leaves you, the lens-cover is always off. I argue for that your camera should always be turned on whenever you carry it in your hand – some argue that the battery can take that kind of handling. The get some extra batteries!

The way you prepare is the way your images will come out! If you miss out on preparations you will probably end up making a lot of images you know deep inside that you could have done better. That is a sad evolution and we know there is a quick remedy to that! Prepare!

Everything we do in general might come out way better. You know that and there are ways to accomplish that without becoming a total control freak. Even if control can't be overrated, it mustn't guide all of your photographic endeavors, but it is never a waste of time. To be safe is to never be sorry. You already knew that, right?

On editing

The way you proceed with a more consistent approach will determine how much you progress in doing different kinds of shoots. The manner in which you edit your images may change over time, but now and again, try to edit older images in another manner.

You might be surprised at what you'll encounter. Images you thought were decent might turn into almost awesome. It might even turn out the other way, the images you thought were borderline awesome a couple of years ago, will turn out without anything interesting in them.

So, it's your mission to find a decent way to edit them. The question you'll put to yourself is why on earth didn't you edit all of your old images with some kind of skill? This is a hard one to answer, there are so many factors influencing the outcome of editing. Rest assured that all images doesn't do well with the same kind of editing. Some will need more contrast, or sharpening, others need other treatments You might have become wiser and more skilled nowadays. You might have developed the necessary skills to develop your images, giving them the treatment they deserve, and thus, bringing out their awesomeness.

In some images there is nothing until you edit them, even a slight crop may work wonders to a seemingly mediocre image. The slight crop may make it stand out. You might still have the 'casting-tunnels' in the original image. When you edit them out, the image appears to become great.

You decide how much editing you do, some will edit, but in a manner that makes it hard to trace that editing, it is done in a rather timid way. The image is enhanced whether you do little editing, or if you go all in. Some go all in with highlighting, sharpening and contrast. You really don't see that the image is so heavily 'manipulated', but it is treated with a whole lot of filters, with the original image in the distance looking like a mere sketch. At least if you compare it to the final, treated image.

As long as we don't argue that this is an image depicting 'reality' it's okay to do 'serious' editing. Be sure that you use only copies of the original – you might want to try a different approach to this image later.

But, if editing isn't what you are interested in, go for some light editing, some unsharp masking, some contrast and cropping out disturbing stuff along the edges of the images. That's format 1A. some may argue that everything beyond that is over editing.

You choose how you edit. No one else is your mama there. You're totally responsible for your own work. It is a drag to experiment, but when you go over the edge and your images are all aboard editing – almost on the brink of using the same frame and doing 20 separate edited versions that the spectator can't recognize as stemming from the same file. You're out there in 'Art land', where nobody can help you – you are totally on your own – and in 'Art land' no one can hear you scream!

Well, that might be uncalled for, but you have a vision of what is limiting what you are doing. And thus, what kind og image you want to present.

Try to envision that idea in a dozen of images – just doing them out for yourself. Try to edit them in the way you envision these images ought to be edited. Let your images rest for a couple of weeks and then, take a new look at them.

Do your images still appeal to your taste? Alright, go ahead and do a couple of dozens in the same style, then let the pictures rest awhile and then, have a go at printing them. Look at the prints. Did they match what you envisioned for this batch of images, or are you now regretting that you started this exercise?

It's hard to be absolutely sure, isn't it? Do you long to show your images to somebody? Are you sure who you're gonna pick as your initial spectator and judge? Why not? Don't you know someone that dare tell you if these images are pure garbage, or not? Probably, that is the problem, there are too many self-proclaimed 'experts' (I'm obviously one of them) who think they know everything there is to know about photography.

The main problem with that kind of attitude being widely spread is that it is not in the eyes of the producer that the image is done and established. It is in the eye of the 'beholder' (who mustn't have a degree in Art History, or Photography) to understand what you are trying to express with your images. The spectator looks at the image and into the image.

That is all.

No need to read explanations, or listen to tales about the 'emotions' of the images. The images are there, right in front of your nose. There is no name for it – gaze at them, get affected – or don't!

You have to develop some kind of style. I've noticed that my photography friends always call my attempts at creating a n expression for a 'manner', but established photographers, even from 'Art land'. Are described as having a 'style'. It is hard to understand what they are really conveying by that. Okay, I don't make my living from photography – I'm in that sense an amateur-hobbyist.

But, really, a 'manner', I like to think of my way of expressing myself as a 'style', but I'm much for arguing with a lot of people having strong opinions about stuff they really haven't congested to its full extent. Let's take some photos, and let the loudmouths keep on talking!

In the course of events you will stumble over ideas that seem sound. You might want to make images of some motifs that will make your images looking like they are trying to copy someone else's images.

That might happen when you focus on motifs like glass, leaves, loosely woven fabrics, or ice. Try that! Try that, even if your inspiration was a photo book about that kind of material! There is no reason to try something you think is interesting just because it has been done by others. You can do it too, but with another twist – adding you stuff to the subject.

If you chose ideas to work on that you think has never even been done before you're in for a long, sad and disappointing road. You have to be prepared on that everything has been done before. Try to develop what has been done, rather than just chasing after that exclusive motif (remember, it seems exclusive just because YOU haven't seen it before. Look at what is happening to street photography – in some circles it is becoming more and more staged every day. People go to exotic places to make 'exotic' images, I reckon that this is no challenge – the real challenge is to make 'exotic' images in your own backyard. You don't have to travel to discover new worlds! You have to practice the art of seeing! Or, maybe, practice the art of finding the art in what you see!

If you look at people who 'matter' in the 'photographic' scene you will find that they, like athletes, practice their skill set, that is, their gaze, to perfection, so that they can locate some new ideas within the everyday life their leading. Photography is firstly about 'gazing', way down on the list comes shutter speeds and lens brands. Try to find your targets within the ordinary, the impact of images make in that manner will have a far greater impact than forced 'exotism' that may seem novel, but rather is a proof of lacking experience.

If you're not interested you don't have to check it out. Everything is out there, around the corner, for the ones who are interested. There's the stuff to take a closer look at, since what can be better than images from speedway races, that you love, especially in the rain. There is the forlorn suburbia with people keeping on living their lives while you see them in the subway car. It's like when I show you images of my kids and relatives. You're polite and watch some, but then you get impatient, and want to move on. To be honest I don't watch the images of my relatives regularly either. I have more important stuff to spend my time with.

Writing this section on a three hour trip with a ferry to the Swedish mainland after I spent a couple of days making images in Visby, the main city in the island of Gotland. Some of the time I spent participating in a photo walk with some locals. Somebody in that group uttered that there are people who think that you don't make good images when walking together in a group like that. "I'm one of those people" said I, "but I think you have to a little social at times too!"

I don't run to every opportunity to do photo walks. Just now the captain of this vessel told us via the speaker system than a helicopter is going to land on the ferry as an exercise. A couple of years ago I would have been talking to the crew now to see if I could make some images of that helicopter exercise. Now I don't care, I'm tired and I want to go home, go to bed and sleep. It's a good three hours left until I am home, I'm afraid.

So, I keep on writing about photography, rather than making images – how sad isn't that?

Literature

Barthes, Roland.1982. *Camera lucida: reflections on photography.* 1st American pbk. ed. New York: Hill and Wang.

Berggren, Uffe. 2018. *Balsamerad tid: fotografiet i den postfotografiska eran.* Stockholm: BoD - Books on Demand.

Berggren, Uffe. 2020. *Embalmed time: photography in the post photographic era.* Stockholm: BoD - Books on Demand.

Doisneau, Robert & Gautrand, Jean-Claude (2003). *Robert Doisneau, 1912-1994.* Köln: Taschen.

Higgins, Jackie. 2013. *Why it does not have to be in focus: modern photography explained.* London: Thames & Hudson.

Mitchell, W. J. T. 2005. *What do pictures want?: the lives and loves of images. Chicago: University of Chicago Press.*

Riesman, David. 1955. *The lonely crowd: a study of the changing by American Character.* New York: Doubleday Anchor Books.

Other sources

Guiness Book of World Records. August 25, 2020. https://www.guinnessworldrecords.com/world-records/first-voice-recording